WHEELSONG POETRY ANTHOLOGY 5

Edited by

Steve Wheeler
Charlene Phare
Brandon Adam Haven

First published by
Wheelsong Books
United Kingdom

© Wheelsong Poetry, 2024

The right of all featured poets to be identified as the authors of this work have been asserted by them in accordance with the Copyright, Designs and Patents Act of 1988.

Cover photo © Steve Wheeler, 2024
Book design and layout © Steve Wheeler, 2024
First published in 2024

All rights reserved. Except as permitted under current legislation no part of this work may be photocopied, stored in a retrieval system, published, performed in public, adapted, broadcast, transmitted, recorded or reproduced in any form or by any means, without the prior permission of the copyright owners. Any enquiries should be addressed to Wheelsong Books.

Softcover Print ISBN: 979-8-34065-120-4

*"A poet is like a nightingale, who sits in darkness
and sings to cheer its own solitude
with sweet sounds."*

—Percy Bysshe Shelley

FUNDRAISING IN AID OF

Save the Children

Foreword

In front of you is Wheelsong Poetry Anthology 5. This is the latest collection of work by poets from six continents. It has been curated with the support of members of several Facebook poetry groups including Wheelsong Poetry, Invisible Poets, Poetry UK, Pure Poetry and Safe Haven. This time, 130 poets donated their poetic works to raise funds for a very worthy cause. This is a creative community and we stand together in support of children in dire need. Our strapline remains: 'Poetry Against Poverty'

Recently I saw two rather naïve questions in Invisible Poets. They were asked by someone who had clearly just arrived in the group. He asked 'Is it a good thing to be published by Wheelsong? Does everyone that submits get published?' The answer to the first questions is, yes – it's a *very good thing* because we band together as a community to save little lives. The answer to the second is, no, of course not. Invariably, fewer than half the submissions are actually selected to appear in a Wheelsong anthology.

As the editors of this volume, Charlene, Brandon and I read through almost 500 submissions, in a rigorous editorial selection process, to bring you a book of almost 250 of the very best poems that celebrate the creative talents of the members in our online poetry groups. Every poem featured in this book has earned its right to be here.

I hope you enjoy this book and that it inspires as well as entertains you. Be assured that by purchasing your copy, you have played your part in helping children who are in desperate need.

Poets against poverty. That's who we are.

Steve Wheeler
Editor in Chief
Poet and founder
Wheelsong Books

Contents

Foreword	Steve Wheeler (EIC)	9
Her Words	Stephen W. Atkinson	19
Red Poppy Hill	Sarah Joy Holden	20
Solar Flares	Kris Fisher	20
Comes a Time	Kevin Francis	21
The Camel Librarian	David C. Grantz	22
Wilting Serotonin	Aoife Cunningham	23
She Blooms	Lorna Caizley	24
Women's Cycles	Shirley Rose	24
The Woman in the Black Dress	Natalie Miller	25
The Whole Week Through	Chuck Porretto	26
The Sixth Month	Karin J. Hobson	27
Muse to Me	Mark Gott	27
Kindness	Marian Dunham	28
The Memory of You	Joan Audette	28
A New Day	Tom Watkins	29
Comfort	Paul Barratt	29
Petals in the Wind	Dusty Gibson	30
Lost Poets	Fouzia Sheikh	31
the midnight darkness	D. A. Simpson	32
Catching Violet	Autumn Burniston	32
Blue Moon Blues	Mark Gott	33
Kandinsky's Synesthesia	Linda Adelia Powers	34
A Forgotten Gift	William Odell	34
Angels	Sharon Toner	35
Dream	Bruce Stewart Hart	35
A Bullfrog's Croak	Emile Pinet	36
It's a Shame	Aoife Cunningham	37
Jackdaws and Nightingales	Mark Heathcote	38
Not a Sound	Emile Pinet	38
Paris	Neil Vincent Scott	39
The Great Fear	David C. Grantz	40
Whether the Weather	Chuck Porretto	41
Loitering Wings	Rafik Romdhani	42
The Symphonies of Somewhere	Autumn Burniston	43
Braving it Out	Terry Bridges	43

Wheelspins	Charlene Phare	44
Grieving	Steve Wheeler	44
Whispering Eyes of Attention	William Odell	45
Diviner	Linda Adelia Powers	45
Blazing	Catherine MacKenzie	46
Be	Jon Thomas	46
The Sound of Rain	Janet Tai	48
Rohese	Fia Aella	49
A Coalescence of Sparks	Emile Pinet	49
The Star	Felista N. Gichia	50
Listening to the Rain	Karen Bessette	50
As Winter Ends	Richard Harries	51
For Deb	Sandra Humphrey	52
Discombobulated	Robert D. Taylor	53
So Far Distant	Brandon A. Haven	53
What Once Stood	D. L. Lang	54
steppingstones	Deborah G. Howard	54
Through all My Long and Time-Spun Years	Valerie Dohren	55
Breakfast Whispers	Fouzia Sheikh	56
He Sent Her Poems	Ken Green	57
God's Gift	Dusty Gibson	57
Oblivious internment of The Psyche's Demise	Brandon A. Haven	58
Inculpable	Gavin Prinsloo	59
Honey Jar	Emily Vanseizenberg	60
This Time	Kevin Francis	60
Bipolar Bard	Steve Wheeler	61
Azure	Fouzia Sheikh	62
I Will Always Remember	Victoria Puckering	63
melt	Deborah G. Howard	63
The Stillest Night	Jon Thomas	64
Footsteps Down the Lane	Kevin Francis	65
For the Children	Michael D. Turner	66
Baptism	Kris Fisher	67
I Just Love to Write	Joe R. Mendoza	67
Unquiet Numbers	Iain Strachan	68
My Heart is like a Tattooed Sleeve	Sharon Toner	69
It's Not Her Mouth	Rafik Romdhani	70
Self-Pity	Kevin W. McNelis	71

Bliss	A. E. Carey	72
My Brain is a Jailer	James Hurst	72
Why Do I Wake?	Brendan Curran	73
The Plan	Nadia Martelli	73
All that Remains	Archie Papa	74
Shall Nature Be	Andy Reay	74
From Absolute Zero	Peter Rivers	75
Perseverance	James Hurst	76
My Message	Richard Harvey	77
Tomorrow's Child	Mike Turner	77
Yesterday's River	Mike Rose	78
The Boys of Sorrow	Sinazo Zoe Ngxabani	79
The Sorrow of Clouds	Tyrone M. Warren	80
Mandalas	Tanya Raval	81
Priceless	Simon Drake	81
Everything and Nothing	Archie Papa	82
Paradise	A. E. Carey	82
A Bond No-one can Break	Kirsty Howarth	83
Quickening Pulse of Lovely Things	Kate Cameron	84
Dark Waters	Kate Cameron	84
Awe	A. E. Carey	85
Spring's Derail	Karin J. Hobson	86
Whispers of Yesterday, Echoes of Life	Lorna McLaren	87
Bedroom	Haytham Trueheart	88
Heaving Breath	Imelda Zapata Garcia	88
Sleep Well Tonight	Valerie Dohren	89
Strangers Friends Lovers	Simon Drake	90
Ghosts Define Us	D. L. Lang	91
Of Silver	Andy Reay	92
The Weeping Willow	Natalie Miller	93
Opportune	Gregory R. Barden	94
Croaking Mind to Mind	Rafik Romdhani	95
Wind of Change	Lorna McLaren	95
The Weeping Tree	Dale Parsons	96
I Danced	Sean Timms	96
The Silhouette's Freedom	Donna Marie Smith	97
Death and Ego	Tanya Raval	97
The Yellow Road	Thomas B. Maxwell	98
the sower of seasons	D. A. Simpson	99

Your Arms and Mine	Brendan Curran	100
Antique	R. D. Fletcher	101
I'll Take Any Crumbles	Jessica Magalhães	102
Along the Path	Archie Papa	102
Sailing Cupid's Sting	Peter Rivers	103
Birdsong	Cypress Land	103
Poetry is My Way to Authenticity	Haytham Trueheart	104
Childhood Jubilation Massacred	Brandon A. Haven	104
These Steps	Anita Chechi	105
Passions of the Heart	Julie Loonat	105
En Pointe	Annie Mitchell	106
Beneath the Broken Skies	Steve Wheeler	107
Tomorrow	Bruce Stewart Hart	107
Mommy, Daddy, is there Something Wrong with Me?	Richard Harvey	108
My Soulmate the Herring Gull	Graeme Stokes	109
Ghost Town	Martha M. Miller	110
Zombie	R. D. Fletcher	110
Flock of Words	Mike Rose	111
Writing Brings Me Back	Natasha Browne	112
Empathetic Souls	Melissa Davilio	113
Incubation	Martha M. Miller	113
The Quintessential Beauty	Brian Benton	114
What is a Poem?	Joan Audette	115
Paws for Effect	Sarah Sansbury	115
Invisible Poet Girl	Jamie Willis	116
Cobweb Days	Sean Timms	117
Cigarra	Imelda Zapata Garcia	118
Do You Feel Me?	Graeme Stokes	119
There Are No Words	Kevin W. McNelis	120
This House	Lorna Caizley	121
Yearning to Run	Linda Adelia Powers	121
Where Have You Gone?	Joan Audette	122
Love Never Grows Old	Sheila Grenon	123
Flowers	Patti Woosley	123
The First Leaf of Autumn	Paul Williams	124
You Don't Belong to Me	Dashaun Snipes	125
At War with My Pen	Natasha Browne	127
Nam Hnub	Cypress Land	128
Opening Doors	Dale Parsons	128

Empty Shell	Brian Benton	129
Let Me Sleep and Dream about England	Jessica Magalhães	130
Garbutt's Map	Iain Strachan	131
Frangere	Cypress Land	132
Burden	Jyothi Bhagawat	133
Frost Smoke	Martha M. Miller	134
My Truth's All Wrong	Nadia Martelli	134
Lines or Less	Ted Gistle	135
Messages of Madness	Peter Rivers	135
Reflections on the Shadows of Adversity	Neil Forsyth	136
Surrender	Susanne West	137
Colouring the Wind	Jyothi Bhagawat	138
Wordslinger	Martin Attard	139
Red September	Jamie Willis	140
I Want to Go	Jyothi Bhagawat	141
The Offering	Larry Bracey	142
you are my oasis	Matthew Elmore	142
The Origin	Michael Balner	143
Sturgeon Moon	Jamie Willis	144
Rage	R. D. Fletcher	144
Children...	Linda Falter	145
October Air	Joseph Gallagher	145
The Reason I Come Home	Larry Bracey	146
Celestial Dance	Paula Rowlands	147
Between the Lines of Time	Linda Falter	148
End of Day	Terry Bridges	149
From the Spectre of the Storm	Neil Forsyth	149
Butterfly	Michelle Tarbin	150
Hoot Owl	Mike Rose	151
Dancing In The Dark	Kirsty Howarth	152
I apologize to my pillow	Matthew Elmore	153
Shipwrecked	Ted Gistle	153
Resurrected Poets	Gavin Prinsloo	154
Existence is Just Existential	David C. Grantz	155
Save the Children	David Parazino	156
In a Daydream	Nick Walker	157
As the River Follows the Sea	Natalie Miller	158
I Am A Poem	Valerie Dohren	159

Love Letters in the Stars	Larry Bracey	160
The Palace in the Valley	Nick Walker	161
The Tree	Darren Power	161
The Downs	Martin Attard	162
Treasure	Sarah Sansbury	163
Show Me The Light	Joseph Sawallisch	163
Shadows	Sarah Wheatley	164
Moon Song	Gregory R. Barden	165
Beach Glass In My Hand	Neal Klein	166
Enter	Susanne West	166
Love	Wayne Riley	167
Bleed	Byron Hawkinson	168
Lavender Lullabies	Melissa Davilio	168
Great Waste	Joseph Andrew Miller	169
Snow Snakes	Matthew Burgio	169
Waterborne	Corey Reynolds	170
The Speed of Sound	Paul Welsh	170
Garlands	Ryan Morgan	171
Of Course	Ted Gistle	171
The Eyes of a Bridge that Sleeps	Donna Marie Smith	172
Mesmerizing	Nan DeNoyer	172
Greyhound	Michelle Tarbin	173
The Essential Stitch	Ryan Morgan	174
Inflating Life	Jodeci Flores	175
Soul Cleansing	Phillip Burgio	175
When The Night is Empty	Martin Attard	176
The Strange Sympathy of Pendulums and Fireflies	Joseph Gallagher	177
Mind Set	Nicholas S. Leslie	178
Embodied	Neal Klein	179
Warm Mangroves	James Garrels	180
It Takes Two to Tango	Melissa Davilio	180
Colors Within	Hannah Gray	181
Rebirth	Sarah Wheatley	182
Color of My Soul	Rose Marie Streeter	183
War in Pieces	Neal Klein	183
Abundance	Lana Martin	184
As You Are	Michael Balner	185
The Sea	Kirsty Howarth	185
Folds of Time	Andy Reay	187

The Maker's Memoir	Jodeci Flores	188
34 Kisses	Lana Martin	189
The Tangerine Dream	Paul Welsh	190
A Poet Made In December	Jou Wilder	191
Words Fail Me	Charlene Phare	191
a sky in fuchsia	D. A. Simpson	192
Echoes	Gavin Prinsloo	193
Under Your Eyelids	Michael Balner	194
The Unseen Presence of Love	Julie Loonat	195
Shattered	Charlene Phare	195
Two by Two	Paul Barrett	196
Washed Away	The Madd Raven	197
The Sky is a Shade of Forever	Chuck Porretto	198
Mercy	Lonnie Budro	199
To Need More Time	Matthew Burgio	200
There's a Giant Slug in Mummy	Alyson Wilson	200
October Moon	Rose Marie Streeter	202

Her Words
Stephen W. Atkinson

Her thoughts
fell like petals
So softly upon
parchment

Turning scribbles
into blossom
Full of wonder
and enchantment

Her blood became ink
Her heart, a beating scroll
Sonnets were her tears
Weeping from her soul

From her lips, a couplet
A stanza's sweet caress
Inhaling words, exhaling verse
Poetry made flesh!

Red Poppy Hill
Sarah Joy Holden

Red poppy on the hill
Where the soldier fell
He who obeyed the call
A valiant sacrifice for all
His name written on a wall
On reflection — men stand still
Amidst poppies on his hill.

Solar Flares
Kris Fisher

The temperature rises
like solar flares
in my mind
I pray for cooling
like the planet
prays for life
I know the sound
of breathing out the fear
inhaling love
that knows
no bounds
It's all I can do
to know the way
Time invades
a wayward soul
waiting for reconciliation
My heart beats
with the sound
of a distant drum
I know the rain
that falls like forgiveness
It's my destiny
I am safe
I am known
It is true
and beautiful
Forever rising
with hope
with knowing
I'm okay
in all this mess
of life
reborn

Comes a Time
Kevin Francis

I used to walk beside you
Happy to let you do the thinking
The acoustic guitar chords
Lifted me out of my skin
And folded me like fresh linen
Safely on the shelf
looking at the entire world
Through a keyhole
A solitude embraced me
Pushed love into my heart
Until I knew what it was to be lonely
Knew it like my own features
And there comes a time
When we have to answer the door

Poured into the rest of it
Diluted my innocence
Year by year, I yearned
Impelling me to learn more
Looking for answers
And taking my chances
But none of those roads go back
You can never return to him
He lays alone every night
I can no longer see him
But I know he is there
sometimes I dream
And there comes a time
When it's all you have

The Camel Librarian
David Catterton Grantz

Upon a log along the sandy path,
Pigtails wagging in Ethiopian gusts,
The young girl waited for the library.
Today she might be the only one,
For a storm front was lifting Saharan
sand, tanning the cloudless sky.

Yet she knew that her librarian would
Persevere, for she led the camel train
That brought enchantment to children
All along her track, undulating among the
Ever-shifting dunes like heaving oceans.

Meanwhile she'd revisit the heartbreak
From one of her novels, when a fisherman
had watched sharks devour his marlin.
Such beauty in struggle — like hers, she thought.
It reminded her of Sisyphus and his rock from
The Greek mythology she'd read last month.

And then the librarian came, her face swaddled
Against the strafing sand, her stoic camels
Leaning instinctively into the gale.
Today they'd shelter beside the school
Where more children waited, as the librarian
Pulled back her several layers of scarves.

Her raven hair tumbled soft onto her shoulders,

While she began watering the dusty camels.
Then she unrolled the rope ladders,
While two-by-two, the children aligned
For the climb up to their treasure.

Wilting Serotonin
Aoife Cunningham

What is the point of memories
if they are just kept in storage?
Fragments of my conscience
littering my brain.
A painter fatigued by the colour grey.
Tears seeps into my pillowcase
with the lack of colour.

Trapped inside photographs,
I attempt to resuscitate youth
Spark a candle for the girl I once knew.
But she died, long ago, born anew.

I am but mere history,
A flame of fiery ferocity
and 'psychiatry' they called it.
Am I lost in the labyrinth of a mystery?

Or insanity?

I was a malfunctioning machine.
Now I am
Sad and
buried.
Wilting
Serotonin.

She Blooms
Lorna Caizley

Within reach, she can see the surface
Permeating through bleakest soil
Warming rays penetrate deep.
Moisture nourished roots press
On, growth ignited
Emerged darkness
Finally,
Now she
Blooms.

Women's Cycles
Shirley Rose

A woman's blood is not always hers
It's life itself given for her to ferry
To spur and spawn another life
Filled with more life-giving blood
And so the cycle turns

A woman's sweat is not always hers
It's work itself learned for her to carry
To earn and burn another job
Filled with more free-flowing sweat
And so the cycle burns

A woman's tears are not always hers
It's death itself come to bury
To take away and separate
Filled with pain and loss and tears
And so the cycle yearns

The Woman in the Black Dress
Natalie Miller

I see her, staring out the window,
Tonight, the wind is a gentle caress,
In silence, she watches the falling snow,
The woman in the black dress

Tears of a fleeting sorrow,
Leave silver whispers upon her cheek,
Here today, and gone in the morrow
She puts her head in her hands and doesn't speak

Do not wilt, poor flower!
I know your pain is beyond the scope,
I see your petals draining of their color,
But where there is life, there is always hope

The raven came, but he did not stay,
His black gaze of depths I cannot fathom,
Please, I cannot bear to see you live your life in grey!
Do not tread so closely to that familiar chasm

Never forget your courage,
Even if your strength is a hollow throne,
You'll find a new sun if you can cross that bridge,
No one should have to face the world alone.

The Whole Week Through
Chuck Porretto

Won't you be my Monday girl.
Oh, it will be a fun day, girl.
The week is young, the day is new,
and when it's done, we won't be through.

For won't you be my Tuesday girl.
A hit the road and cruise day, girl.
The weather's fair, the sky is blue,
Let's feel the air come rushing through.

Then won't you be my Wednesday girl.
A very best of friends day, girl.
A nature park, an ocean view,
and when it's dark, we won't be through.

And won't you be my Thursday girl.
A spend a his and hers day, girl.
We'll saunter down the avenue,
as city sounds are floating through.

Oh, won't you be my Friday girl.
A never say goodbye day, girl.
My love for you is strong and true.
The week at hand is hardly through.

So be my girl on Saturday.
A nothing else will matter day.
Some music, art, a café too,
but when we part, we won't be through.

Please won't you be my Sunday girl.
though never only one day, girl.
A single day will never do,
I pray you'll stay the whole week through.

A month, a year, will never do,
I need your love my whole life through.

The Sixth Month
Karin J. Hobson

How can death be compared to summer?
Who counts in seconds asking why?
Sorrow is mankind's, not Heaven's;
His contradictions to a sinner's cry!
Secrets belie each mortal man;
Let no one condemn nor deny,
Charge assists with overt concern,
as Truth shall man by comply;
Venomous snake shall take a life,
Perspective has not been lost;
Communications albeit wilfully sly,
Spoke volumes to he at any cost;
Let palms gently sway in summertime air,
Permitting eagles to death dive and compete;
Enjoy the sixth month era of Life's declare,
In the hour of our finest retreat.

Muse to Me
Mark Gott

"Fool," said my muse to me, the pleasure of my pain,
"Look into your heart" and write.
In every fresh shower of my sundried brain,
Write with fervor, words pure and bright.
Let your words flow freely, from your soul's deep core,
Express the depths of what you have, forevermore.
Don't bite your truant pen, beating yourself in spite
Poetry forever comes forth to entertain.
"For in your heart, lies the truest light."

Kindness
Marian Dunham

We can't hold kindness to us,
It's something that must be shared
We don't to have brag about it,
What we do need not be aired.

We can do our good deeds quietly,
We do not have to tell,
There is no need for pomposity,
We do not have to yell.

If everyone did little acts
Of kindness every day,
And every kindness was passed on
We'd all have our part to play.

What a better world we'd live in,
One of which we could be proud,
Where everyone showed little acts
Of kindness to the crowd.

The Memory of You
Joan Audette

In the attic of my mind
stored remembrances of you,
amidst yellowed love letters
tied in faded blue.

Through the lace curtains,
blows a breeze of things anew;
yet on the air, a gentle scent...
the memory of you.

A New Day
Tom Watkins

The silence
of the crashing waves
pulls the sun
from the ocean floor
to illuminate a new day,
a new beginning
for the entire world
Slowly the waves
erase yesterday's footsteps
A fresh palette
for us to paint is created
The possibilities are as endless
as our collective imaginations
This morning
opened my eyes early
to this day
The rising sun warms me
as I embrace the possibles
A new day has risen
elevating tranquil hope

Comfort
Paul Barrett

There's nothing like a corned beef hash
to soothe a soul on winter nights.
Those fatty strings of meat with mash
say nothing's like a corned beef hash.
Though any meal would be a smash
when Mother gets the gravy right,
there's nothing like her corned beef hash
to soothe a soul this winter night.

Petals in the Wind
Dusty Gibson

Millions of bright stars were sprinkled
all across a black to navy gradient tranquil night sky.
Nevertheless, this was not what ended up
drawing my exceedingly inquisitive eye.
The yellowy ethereal glow of the full moon
loomed large over top.
The intoxicating floral fragrant scents
were what first caused me to stop.

I felt titillated by the sensual heady aroma
when it blew in with the gentle wind.
I heard the euphonious sounds of the ocean
while picturing beautiful red roses in my mind.
Right after I'd begun sauntering along the balcony I spied
Thick crimson rose petals dancing
an amazingly effortless glide.

I glanced down at the exuberant dolphins
playing in the ocean below,
as I watched the rose petals pivot
and spiral during their boisterous show.
I was so captivated by the roses' elegant natural act.
They became all I desired to be conscious of
as a matter of fact.

The bold petals glided in the energetic breeze,
performing acrobatics as upon a trapeze.
Petals were swaying and swinging
with delightful aromatic graceful agility.
Their unchoreographed dancing harmonious
with Mother Nature's capability.
However these petals in the wind came to me,
they reminded me how thrilling it is to be free.

Lost Poets
Fouzia Sheikh

Once many beautiful
souls came here to share
Their words of beauty,
love and despair
From every corner
of the world they'd write
Pouring out their hearts
with all their might.

Their words would weave a tapestry
Of human life and history,
But lately, something strange
Had occurred
All those souls started to disappear
Their voices unheard.

No more verses
From those who once wrote,
No more stories, no more tales
Their words have faded into the night
And their absence leaves us
Without light.

What had happened
To those lost poets
We may never know
Perhaps their hearts grew weary,
And they had to go.

But their legacy still lives on,
In the words they've penned.
Their voices still echo in our hearts.

the midnight darkness
D. A. Simpson

the midnight darkness
yielded to the unseen hand
studding the firmament

with a million lights
garnered from the eternal treasury
where light unquenchable abides

as the night hour
supreme did reign

amid myriad upon myriad mysteries
abounding in an unfathomable sky

while a moon of ivory
hung low 'gainst the violet backdrop
adorned by a tableau of dark boughs
etched upon the celestial canvas

a world within worlds

Catching Violet
Autumn Burniston

I heard you gasp as
it cut through the quiet
I felt the blood in my bones to my cheeks
Catching violet
For a second I'm
convinced you could
Sell me a sigh and I'd buy it
Your skin like milk below the moon
And under you, my violet

Blue Moon Blues
Mark Gott

Underneath the pale blue moonlight,
I'm feeling oh, so low.
Got the blue moon blues tonight,
Can't seem to let them go.
Been walking for miles, with the weight of my mistakes,
Shadows grow longer, as my spirit aches.
Blue moon shining in the sky,
All I feel is pain inside.
I'm singing the blue moon blues,
Lost in this heartache, paying my dues.
Memories like shadows in my mind,
Haunting me with every step I take.
I'm searching for love I can't find,
In this endless, lonely heartbreak.
Under the blue moon, I'm feeling so alone.
The stars are shining brightly,
but I can't find my way home.
The world is spinning 'round me, but I'm standing still,
In this blue moonlight, can't help but feel the chill.
Blue moon, won't you set me free,
From this aching in my heart, and the chains that bind me.
I'm singing the blues under your watchful gaze,
Blue moon, shine on me, light up my weary days.
The world keeps on turning, but I'm stuck in the past,
I'm reaching for something, but it's slipping through so fast.
In the stillness of the night, I pray for a sign,
To break free from this sorrow, and leave my blues behind.
I pray for my savior, he'll lead me through the night,
In this blue moonlight, I'm searching for a guiding light.
In the arms of the night, I'll find my way
With your gentle glow, I'll face another day.
Blue moon, guide me through and help me to choose,
To leave behind these blues, in your calming, healing hues.

Kandinsky's Synesthesia
Linda Adelia Powers

The blues are our spirits
    the birds of the sky
        our minds wishing for peace
The greens are our nature
    forests reaching for light
        our souls growing in life
The yellows and pinks are our arts
    wildflowers flooding a field
        our selves finding our hands
The blacks and whites are our reason
    nights and days in equation
        our senses writing logical music
The reds are our passions
    lava flowing down
        our hearts yearning for love

A Forgotten Gift
William Odell

Another
day in the Time vault
another
withdrawal of breaths —

Many blessings to count
and deposit

as you tiptoe along the edge
of the outgoing tide
while memorizing
the last few riffs —

from the Sun

Angels
Sharon Toner

Don't let the angels come and get me
Cos I'm not ready yet
I know they need the good people
They want humanity, to represent
Just because I'm a little tired
And have suffered a lot of pain
Please don't come and get me yet
Cos there's still something, I need to do
So please show a little mercy
Upon my soul today
I beg of you, please dear angels
Let me stay another day
You see my mother's heart
Well, it will break in two
So understand, today
Is just a little too soon
She needs to see me smile
A few more times, at least
So she can hold that smile
In her treasured memories
For those days and weeks to come
When I'm no longer here
So please listen to my prayer
Don't let the angels come and get me
Cos I'm not ready yet.

Dream
Bruce Stewart Hart

Drifting into midnight
I keep returning to a dream..
From what they call reality
To what I'd have it seem

But I know the real illusion
Lay somewhere, in-between.

I dream throughout the darkness
And am soon to face the dawn..
Will the dream make rhyme or reason
Or between the two, will I be torn?

Never to be an answer
To this question, too forlorn..
For I know the real illusion
Began the moment I was born.

A Bullfrog's Croak
Emile Pinet

Silent as smoke, darkness descends;
as shadows merge and daylight ends.
For summoned by a bullfrog's croak;
darkness descends, silent as smoke.

The Moon pools in ebony skies;
gilded golden; she starts to rise.
One of the night's brightest jewels;
in ebony skies, the Moon pools.

Blue bleeds red from a dying sun,
a telltale sign that day is done.
Inking crimson clouds overhead;
from a dying sun, blue bleeds red.

Signaling their love, fireflies flash;
as dusk settles like sooty ash.
Under the stars, twinkling above;
fireflies flash, signaling their love.

It's a Shame
Aoife Cunningham

It's a shame that the necessity of living
  comes in a physical form of taking
  our coins and achievements.
  from the hearts of our ancestors.
Why is it expensive to live
  in a world so giving and loving?
Why do we charge for the
  equipment to get to our desired destinations?
We're all going to end up 6 feet under regardless.
Gold is heavy anyways.
Money's a burden that all of us angels carry
  the weight of this greed.
My bank account is in deficit but
  like stones on our back,
  coins and dollars
  still snap my wings.
Why are differences
Painted with sin?
  "by the world's system
  of restriction and exclusion"
"By the hunger of another."
Bounding our free spirits in fear.
Afraid that we'll fall from the height
  of our ambitions. Believe in imagination
      — we can do anything.
Breaking angels wings, blinding sight.
  isn't how we should be.
Just because you don't enjoy this
  figuring out jigsaws ….
  doesn't give you the right to break it into pieces.
Every single human is a piece in this puzzle,
Come together and the image will be beautiful.

Jackdaws and Nightingales
Mark Heathcote

What is momentary today is the laughter of children
their noise fills the air like a humming factory
but tomorrow, I'll feel instantly quite differently
their voices will be like heavenly songbirds
and I will question these two separate reactions
with the same heart that experienced their fracas joys
like Jackdaws one moment and Nightingales the next.
And then my soul will perch on a fence
between two schools of thought for extra legitimate balance.

Not a Sound
Emile Pinet

Look up to a sky full of stars
akin to trillions of diamonds.
And watch a gold doubloon moon climb
high amidst a starlit background.

Not a sound, just you and your thoughts,
all worldly distractions vanish.
And critiquing God's handiwork
your soul binds with humanity.

A sizzling shooting star burns bright,
unzipping a curtain of sparks.
And bats start patrolling for moths,
flapping skin-soft wings as night falls.

Shifting shadows slowly conjoin,
turning charcoal grey into black.
And tattooing twilight phantoms,
dusk, inks day in colors of night.

Paris
Neil Vincent Scott

i once held her
    ever so close
danced with her
    til the first light of dawn
drank her wine
tasted her delicacies
and was adrift in her charms
from montmartre
to the champs-élysées
across her history
from the louvre
to the eiffel tower
the museums
and the memories
from bonjour
    to au revoir
it's 2:30 am
and i'm wide awake
sitting on the side of the bed
staring at a photo of paris
dreaming of a gentler time
now you and she
are revelling in her charms
for yesterday
    she was mine
    for a time
but today
she belongs
    lovingly to you
hold fast to the magical moments
for tomorrow
    she will be gone
that's just the way she is
    paris

The Great Fear
David Catterton Grantz

A slipping tide before tsunamis,
The Great Fear bides his time,
Stroking the feather of his quill.

Says, "They'll never see me coming."

Within these hallowed halls, his
Minions assemble, as he crouches
Before them, sinew rippling.

His pitiless eyes fixed upon his prey
Shall never blink, shall not relent,
As virtue bends before the blade.

Says, "They'll never know what hit them.

Denial stops their ears and blocks
Their eyes, as, like a gasp, my shadow
Slips long the burnished banister."

Fear presides above his caustic screed,
Concocting how best to frame it,
How best to utilize his talents.

"Yes, of course, of course!
It's so obvious to me now!"

He lays the quill aside,
and begins.

Whether the Weather
Chuck Porretto

Whether the weather's a pleasure,
or whether the weather's a pain,
we'll weather the weather together, my treasure,
by tempest or delicate rain.

And whether the weather is foggy,
or whether the weather is clear,
and whether the weather is sullen and soggy,
we'll weather the weather, my dear.

For whether the weather is wind through the heather,
by storm or a warm gentle breeze,
we'll weather the weather forever together,
we'll weather the weather with ease.

And whether the weather is cloudy,
or withered from summery sun,
and whether the weather is raucous and rowdy,
we'll weather the weather as one.

And whether the weather is soft as the feathery
fluff from the heavens above,
or whether the weather is tough as old leather,
we'll weather the weather in love.

Loitering Wings
Rafik Romdhani

You wish to stand in the doorway,
to cast your eye on the winsome
landscape bound to shape.
You would be likely to dream,
drum up dreams as you wake,
turn the corner and head to new hills.
But you need to catch this tabanid fly,
enemy of life and butterflies.
A being conspiring with acerbic dung
to curb your unstoppable eye.
Loitering wings in somersaulting air,
blind to space become sullen traces.
Grind this buzzing, little mind
before it gets through the window
you did leave ajar for vile faces,
before it leaves on your desk
a delirious note about a bloody saw
it will use to drain your blood out.
You wish to stand in the doorway
amidst the frisky air.
You wish to cast your eye on a world
that is not there.

The Symphonies of Somewhere
Autumn Burniston

The symphonies of somewhere
The harmonies of harbours
The Melodies of masons
Who happen to be writers
Who scribe sweet sonatas

For the bards who bark the bay
That give us reason to believe
We'll fall in love someday.

Oh, the symphonies of somewhere
The rhythm of the roads,
The beat that empties bottles,
The lines that lift the loads,
The measures of the moments
The countless kisses in the grey
That give us reason to believe
We'll fall in love someday

Braving it Out
Terry Bridges

Silence travels down the nerves...a cool adrenaline
Smooths out the inconsistencies of a torrid day
Buckets of relief water my sombre reflections
The evening buzzes in the afterglow
I do not care for the clash of steel on stone
Though words are weapons brandished in stale air
Just taunt me and I'll savage your composure
I'll venture like scripture not to bring peace but a sword
Nothing in it of course...acting a false bravado
Shy in my demeanour...erupting inside
Much to be admired in putting on a happy face
Though worries twist spaghetti-like in the mind
So follow me through eternal labyrinths
I'll guide you to gleaming treasure my fellow explorers
Companions of the dark...kin of my kind

Wheel Spins
Charlene Phare

For every car that backfires
And every bike bell that rings
There's method in the madness
As Saturn spins her rings
When answers remain hidden
And connectivity poor
There's nothing to console you
As you can't take anymore
When setting wheels in motion
And time to bring the changes
There's knowledge that you cling to
As your new gear engages
You're driving with conviction
Revelling in the power
Overtaking the slow lanes
Extracting sweet from sour

Grieving
Steve Wheeler

In deepest grief
Shall oil of salving grace be poured
As healing touch holds solace high
For as the memories flood your mind
You shed the tears of bygone times
To measure out your loss

Time is a thief
It robs from each what was adored
But now is lost, to years that fly
So fleet the sweetest days run blind
Time's rolling stone has no more rhymes
Nor does it gather moss

The Whispering Eyes of Attention
William Odell

So
dare I ask
if you feel seen
With hands on hips
decked out
in post-Labor Day white
you chug
the streaming
spotlights of sunshine
gushing
through your requested
cracks in the sky
now afraid
the fiery outbursts —
might wake up the rain

Diviner
Linda Adelia Powers

Slipstream of the ambivalent
Ambient chorus of shifting ambitions
Subliminal moons rising into the clouds
Prancing like sparks in the shallows

Motionless spirals of dreamless sleep
Skyscrapers of memory frozen
Cliffs collapsing in one breath of time
Suns rampant erasing the sky

Kinetic shades diffused from beyond
Dispersal of stories ancient anew
Heads doused with shimmering haloes of dew
Oracles whispering names of the few

Blazing
Catherine A. MacKenzie

I don't tread lightly
Into blazes of fire,
I go
Madly,
Sometimes sadly
Without purpose,
Life has no meaning
At times,
I hear no chimes,
No rhymes
Of comfort,
No rainbow at the end
Of the bend,
Yet...
I still pray
For the fire
To extinguish.

Be
Jon Thomas

Be still in all the chaos
Be love in all the hate
Be serene in all that's mean
Be early with the late.

Be clear in all the shadows
Be light when only dark
Be the truth to the dissolute
Be static when there's sparks.

Be found in all adventures
Be straight on crooked paths
Be the seed that nature needs
Be first in all that's last.

Be fixed to all the broken
Be sober with the drunk
Be support in all the faults
Be open with the shut.

Be different with the normal
Be white within the grey
Be the seen in broken dreams
Be night in every day.

Be the one that's needed
Be freedom to the slaved
Be the key to locked belief
Be convex to concaved.

Be yourself with others
Be there without the why
Be what you need for dignity
Be now not by and by.

Be pathways undiscovered
Be cures for all that bleed
But most of all, be what you know
Be growth, become the seed.

The Sound of the Rain
Janet Tai

Every time it rains
I'll stand out at my
Balcony
Listening to the sound
As it falls accompanied by
The clash of thunder

The dark grey skies
The ferocity of
The rain
Aided by the wind
Never fails to stir up past
Memories

How to forget?
Especially today
My 42nd wedding
Anniversary — bleh!
My 21st year
As a cancer survivor

The rain represents
The volume of tears
Shed in my heart
Over the years
Only a change could make
September feels less bitter

Rohese
Fia Aella

Smell the scent of those there roses,
most beautiful in bloom,
curiously romantic,
ever seductive,
luring plenty to doom.

Glance an eye over bright the palette,
impressive be this view,
yet of the stem,
a prick or two,
many oh shall but rue.

A Coalescence of Sparks
Emile Pinet

The manifestation of God's word,
The Big Bang created the universe,
a phantasmagorical coalescence of sparks.

Billions of galaxies swirl in the fabric of time and space
like filigree clusters set with pulsars and quasars,
their massive black holes, generating cosmic rays.

Harbingers of life and death, stars define infinity;
as black matter anchors gravity's web of threads
blurring boundaries of science and creation
afloat in an unfathomable sea of ebony.

The Star
Felister N. Gichia

It's already past midnight
And I can tell I have lost count
Of the minutes I have been here

It's been a very unusual night
Extremely cold and windy
Layers of the ice covering my body

I have been standing under a tree
My eyes glued to the dark sky
Making a silent prayer to God

I have many wishes to make
But today I'm on a single mission
A mission to spot my 'leading' star

At my giving up point
I hear a whisper from above
Telling me to search no further

For the star is within me
I'm the star that I have been searching for
A leading star to my desired destination

Listening to the Rain
Karen Bessette

Listening to the rain, a memory,
A touch, a dream, a love so deep.
Listening to the rain gently fall,
My heart overflows with wondrous joy.

As Winter Ends
Richard Harries

I walk out in the dark
Use my phone as a torch
And follow the sounds
The sounds at the end of my street
Waves swirling and splashing
Crashing and roaring
I walk across the pathway
That is the promenade
At the end of our street
Where steps lead
down to the beach
To the sea, to the noise
Darkness surrounds me
As I stand looking out
Out towards France
Then gradually a feeling
A feeling of rebirth inside me
As light breaks
Slowly, but magnificently
Illuminating the world around me
I look to the waves, into them
And at the sea,
the whole swirling miasma
The horizon
As light explodes
And lightens my life
Re-energizing me
And my soul, my being

For Deb
Sandra Humphrey

In those dark days
When the sun turned our skin golden
and the dust and straw of bricks
not yet placed coated our shoes.
In that turmoil
In that sadness of long June days spent in fields
and woods in summer's blissful haze.
In that despair
that we as children had not the words to cast into the air.
When loves first rays had touched our tender hearts
and stung like nettles on our shins.
In that sadness
In that grief
We shared our spoils and tears
and dared ourselves to dream.
In those long days of scudding clouds
and skies as blue as the sea that licked our toes.
In those hawthorn heady days of kisses
stolen from boys with lashes and love.
In that dread
the turn for home
the days end
the fading golden light and blackbirds joyful song
we linked our arms and hearts and clung through laughter
and smiles to face the waiting torment.
In that life,
We wore our armour lightly
We wielded swords of hazel that cut away our pain.
In this life,
two women battle worn wise and strong.
Courage nurtured from those harvest fields
from those leafy dens
from secrets shared on childhood battlefields.
Friendship found in days of darkness and innocence
will bind us forever more.

Discombobulated
Robert D. Taylor

Are you confused or maybe befuddled?
Does it make you feel bewildered and muddled?
Do you feel neck deep in a muddy puddle?
Does it perplex and ruffle?
Is it some kind of puzzle?

A word to confound, fluster and addle.
Like being in a boat without a paddle.
Language to baffle, confound, perplex...

Are you discombobulated yet?

So Far Distant
Brandon Adam Haven

I wear deep sadness with a resplendent smile,
Concealed within the tumult of endless desolate trials.
Awaiting to gleam once again in a bleak glowing vision,
Far distant from self-hatred and jaunting derision.
Liberate me, I beseech, from mine useless tears,
For it availeth naught no matter how sincere.
The ephemeral recollections of a pure childhood gone
It's all of decay and so far distant now.
Black is where that child now resides,
Surmounted and suffocated, full of strife.
Imploring for love that's ever disconcerting,
May the world immolate,
I'm weary from hurting....

What Once Stood
D. L. Lang

Here lies the Soviet guard tower that peered over the border
a few miles from the West German town I was born in.
Here lies the ruins of my first elementary school in Louisiana
right beside the now defunct military base that brought me there.
Here lies the ruins of the television station where I used to
volunteer amongst the discarded broadcast licences
of another that paid me.
Somewhere deep inside a landfill lies the historical records
that sparked my interest in the history of what came before.
Here lies the railroad tool house my friends and I explored
and somewhere along the tracks, friendships await rekindling.
Here lies the songs I used to sing with conviction and fervor,
representing identities that I no longer give any power.
It is all just a whisper in winds never meant to be immortal,
so bless those that come before you lest fate close the portal.
Here lies all the friends, colleagues, and family I have outlived.
Within our hearts each place and person survives eternal.

steppingstones
Deborah Griffin Howard

to step upon the grace of Life
to cheat Death one more time
giving up
in despair
of losing you
with nothing to lose
a stepping stone
that I missed
when I was young
in the creek
of everyman

Through all My Long and Time-Spun Years
Valerie Dohren

Through all my long and time-spun years
I've watched the moon full wax and wane
Beheld the oceans ebb and flow —
Walked in the sunshine and the rain

I've glimpsed the flowers bloom in Spring
In Autumn's chill, their petals fall
Known much of happiness and pain
Seen those set low 'neath those stood tall

I've fixed my eyes upon the dawn
Upon the dazzling setting sun
Have thus beheld the glitt'ring stars
In full display when day is done

And in the passing of the years
As earth in all her beauty turns
I've known the seasons marking time
And witnessed every soul that yearns

I've watched the rich man take his fill
The poor man falter in his wake
Known those who walk on fallow ground
And those the world chose to forsake

I've smiled through all my halcyon days
With joy and splendour to abide
But in the darker hours when spent
That's when I've cried, oh how I've cried

So what remains in future years
For such I cannot yet foretell —
Whatever time be left for me
I deem that I shall use it well

Breakfast Whispers
Fouzia Sheikh

The sun cracks through
the sleepy sky,
And birdsong joins
the morning sigh.
A golden glow paints kitchen walls,
As sleep's last tendrils gently fall.
The sleepy kettle hums,
a fragrant thrill, a steamy plume,
As drowsy senses
heed the coffee's thrall.
The coffee brews,
a dark delight,
Its rich aroma takes its flight.
Awaking scents that chase
the gloom.
Of toasted bread,
Eggs that whisper,
"Wake up,"
And jam a jewel,
in sunshine hues,
On warm-kissed toast,
On plates of white,
a canvas bright unfurls,
With buttered toast, a sunlit,
golden frame.
And jewel-toned fruits,
their colours dancing whirls,
a morning muse.
And honey's kiss,
a sweetness soft and slow,
Melts on the tongue,
a gentle morning loop.
In simple fare, a symphony takes flight,
A dance of senses,
bathed in morning light.

He Sent Her Poems
Ken Green

She was never
much the reader
nor him the talker
but he could write

words at high tide
more than the ocean
could ever hold
only for her

read over and over
her heart would burst
teaching of love
never thought possible

she learned to read
what wasn't written
and now he could
speak the words

and still ...
he sends her poems

God's Gift
Dusty Gibson

My existence was not bright
It was shrouded without light
Angels played a joyous horn
Then my baby girl was born
A true gift from God above
I feel more than all-out love
Her precious beauty shining

She is my silver lining
With her in my grey cloud life
There is no more awful strife
She helps me to always cope
My shining light-love-n-hope
I exist within her light
Shining so truly strong-n-bright
God's gift on wings of a dove
Overflowing me with love
Joy, smiles, light, love, hope-n-more
She makes my life not a chore
Her eyes give sun rays of light
She is my rainbow so bright
She is my shining light life
Always and in afterlife

Oblivious Internment of The Psyche's Demise
Brandon Adam Haven

My refuge, concealed in yesterday's pocket
Laden in soft decimation unfolding
Rotting is the scent of my decaying flesh
I beshrew this desecrating pulse, forgotten
Its state frivolous, dripping from tired veins
Its form lost in the ecstasy of my breath
Burning my careless ways to an ashen haze,
Heavily subdued, eyes now peeling away
Breaking pillars through defiant skies
Oblivious internment of The Psyche's Demise

Inculpable
Gavin Prinsloo

The cost is lost as the wings
of change blows trust away,
Time has paused, there are no doors
that can hold the hate at bay

Upon feet of clay a child at play,
she finds no right to mend the wrong,
To gods we pray yet there are no words to say
when the innocent end their song

In love and war we can but adore
the essence of the child,
The silent call when the innocent fall,
the very earth defiled

Shadows on walls and mortality calls,
it is the young who carry the guilt,
Sword and blade and reason unmade,
the cause buried to the hilt

Why the child and their love defiled,
playing war is no children's game,
In truth we rob the innocent of youth;
for in their eyes, there is no blame

Honey Jar
Emily Vanseizenberg

My mind runs, but
my mouth runs faster.
She spills my thoughts
like sweet honey
from a jar, for
everyone to lick.

Before I know it,
the crock is empty
and the world knows
my secrets,
my hopes,
my dreams.

Slowly, my mouth
permeates with a
viscous poison.
I have to drink this,
'cause nobody else will.

Regret tastes bitter.

This Time
Kevin Francis

The time it takes to talk
The time it takes to smile
The time it takes to wink and grin
You should do it all the while

The time it takes to call
The time it takes to sing
The time it takes to dance a jig

The happiness you could bring

The time it takes to be silly
The time it takes to care
The time it takes to sit and listen
And make someone glad you're there

The time it takes to read this
Was not wasted, for you'll see
The smile upon your lips
Is the time you've spent with me

Bipolar Bard
Steve Wheeler

I'm a bipolar bard
I am quiet I am bold
I am up I am down
I blow hot I blow cold
I am angry I'm calm
I am young I am old
I'm a bipolar bard
and I'm far from the fold

My lines are refined
and my writing is wild
I use words like an adult
or a truculent child
you can't count all my formats
my methods and styles
I'm a bipolar bard
a mosaic compiled

I'm a bipolar bard
with a rainbow of rhymes
a confusion of rhythms
a confection of lines

I'm a metaphor muse
in a tempest of times
I'm a bipolar bard
and my oddity shines

Azure
Fouzia Sheikh

Blue sky, so vast and wide
Stretching over land and tide
A canvas of azure hues
Painted with a master's view.
Above our heads it reigns supreme
A kingdom of light and dreams
Where clouds dance and birds soar
And dreams take flight forevermore.

Rolls in, you fogs and pours
out ashen haze
In tattered rays of mist,
Smoother the livid swamp
Of Autumn days.
Frost makes its way
from beyond the azure blue,
Rain pours as heavy as it will please,
passing through a cold winter breeze.

Charming and persistent
Touching our heart and soul
Painting shadows on the sky.
If skies could tell stories,
Tonight it's telling mine.
The orange moulds memories,
Language of love,
Beautiful stories,
But swiftly slithering to mauve.

I Will Always Remember
Victoria Puckering

I remember a time
When your present and mine clashed
Also crashed
You forgot
The friendship we had lost
Never to be regained
As our present never will clash again
Our lost friendship forever ingrained
Life carries on
But never quite the same
Until one day our paths cross again
I will always remember your name

melt
Deborah Griffin Howard

melt me away
like ice cream
that drops and you lick
melt me away
for to be so close
melt me into you
how do you tick
how do you lick
every drop of you
is a new flavor
of us

The Stillest Night
Jon Thomas

Late last night I saw a raven, he was perched upon a post
Silhouetted by the moon, a silver lining ghost
His eyes burnt deep into my soul as I meandered past
Is this raven here to take me, make this day my last.

The caws he gave were haunting, such a deathly melody
Every step and every breath, the raven sowed the seed
Doubts would scurry in my mind,
   my thoughts were on the line
Is this raven here to take me, have I run my time.

A ruffled feather fell below, collected on the floor
I swear the raven said my name then uttered never more
I quickened pace, found shelter, in the leeway of a door
Is this raven here to take me, am I done for sure.

Huddled in the doorway, far removed from raven's gaze
I think back to tales of my younger, youthful days
I recall the stories that my mother used to tell
How my father saw a raven, days before he fell.

This stillest night shone darkly as the raven sang his caw
The fear inside grew brighter, sights
   and sounds not sensed before
Was this apparition a cursed message from our host
Last night I saw a raven who was perched upon a post.

Footsteps Down the Lane
Kevin Francis

Breeze fluttered petals
Dried and slightly bruised
Tumble down paths forgotten
Into oaks and elms and yews
The whole parade, has passed away
Smiles are faded, eyes have failed
And pastel memories look no more
For footsteps down the lane

Hollyhocks strain their stems
A friendly face to see
Those curled up in monochrome
When bees would come to tea
And blackbirds still reminisce
Through the freshly scented rain
Of so many days like this
Of footsteps down the lane

Take my arms, lead me back a way
To the bramble swords of fire
Where we would take our pots
And fill the lot, for the sake of pies
Down leafy walks let us go once more
Amongst the lupins and fleabane
And listen on the breeze
For those footsteps down the lane

For the Children
Michael D. Turner

Let us cry for the children
Those neglected, abused, exploited
Malnourished, sick, uneducated
Made homeless by war
Let us stand for the children
Illuminating their misfortune,
  mistreatment

Those in need of support,
  encouragement, rescue
Shining light on their need
Let us act for the children
Tending to their needs,
  their hopes, their dreams

Food for bodies, succor for souls
Instilling justice, restoring self
For sympathy and empathy
  are not enough

In that they do not alleviate despair
It is rather our action
Which gives meaning
  to our cries and stands
Translating them to relief
Let us cry, let us stand, let us act

For our future
For humanity
For the children

Baptism
Kris Fisher

I'm paying attention
to these beautiful visions
they captivate a radiant center
a grounded sense
the root of expression
the dawn of newness
the patience of evening
the vibration of change
the lines of determination
they're the telling of love
they're the potential
of what will transform us
in peaceful waters
that baptize this moment

I Just Love to Write
Joe R. Mendoza

I don't write for fortune,
I don't write for fame,
I won't use other poets
To help build up my name,
I just love to write, and
I do it just for me.
Whenever I sit down to write
It's because a spirit beckons me.
Poems are sometimes like spirits
That are waiting to be set free.
They live inside of you
And they live inside of me.
And only when the time is right
You'll know when to set them free.
So please don't speak ill of me,

Because I haven't spent my life
Following in your footsteps.
I just write to help me ease my pain.
And my poems may not be worthy
To make me the next poet laureate,
I just write to free these spirits
Whether you like them or not.

Unquiet Numbers
Iain Strachan

In the sun's unquiet numbers, angels see
Writhing arcs of coronal holy flame
Flooding the void with sacred energy
Pregnant with meaning in a weaving game.

Colour and form combine to Edenic play
Kandinsky's art depicts agnostic grace.
In natural patterns, maybe more's to say
An angel's kiss; the freckles on your face.

Orb-like figures from sun on camera lens
Yield spiritual revelations too,
The hues from stained-glass panes,
   bestowed on stones
Are syllables of vision, red and blue.

As pareidolic clouds devour the sun.
So disconnected fragments fuse to one.

My Heart is Like a Tattooed Sleeve
Sharon Toner

I'm an open book
My pages a little worn
Like a little book of words
Defining my heart's core
For here in this book
It's so clear to see

That my heart is like
A tattooed sleeve
As sometimes words
Just paint a picture true
Of everything that lives
Deep inside of me

Every picture entwines
From one to the next
Making up a sleeve
Out of all my history

Interwoven with subtext
So if you could see
My tattooed sleeve
What pictures do you think
You would now see?
For I'm as playful as a kitten
Yet as strong as a lion

My family's like an orange
Peel, pith, segments and pips
My children are in apples in my eyes
My life's pain is there too
In the tears I've shed so many times

Each stitch in every scar
Could never define
The anguish my soul has felt
At certain times in my life

But still I see the beauty
In the morning sunrise
And the beauty of the rose
That's in full bloom

The autumnal overture
As leaves turn to browns and golds
Then the glistening of the snow
Right beneath my feet

And there in each snowflake
That's lands so gently
On my tattooed sleeve
With all its memories it keeps.

It's Not Her Mouth
Rafik Romdhani

That's not her mouth
It's rather two scattered petals
wishing to make one rose
but collided and stuck together
in the hustle and bustle of life.

Self-Pity
Kevin William McNelis

Sadness fills a mason jar
I keep high upon the shelf,
Most every day I feel the need
To go and get it down.
I might choose to take a sip or two
Or chug it like a clown.
Either way the sorrow grows
Until I've had my fill.
Slowly then the tears will fall
Like gentle autumn rain.
And one-by one I'll snatch them up
Into the jar again.
When the jar has reached the brim
I put it back on high,
And save it for tomorrow's thirst
Lest the jar go dry.
Another shelf sits a little higher still,
And holds a glass or two.
Happiness is a shiny green
And Hope's an azure blue.
Oh how I long to drink from those
Higher cups and taste their liquid joy.
But my will and reach are just a little shy,
And I'm such a tired boy.
In the morning perhaps I'll reach them both,
And delight in all their flavor
Tonight instead I'll sip from "Pity's Cup"
And every drop I'll savor!

Bliss
A. E. Carey

Sitting in my garden
Amongst the fragrant flowers
Taking wonders in
Upon this golden hour
Deep in ocean blue
A sky brilliant and sunny
Glimmer flowing strands of hair
Amber and warm like honey
Bees they ever bustle
I feel their delicate hum
It's here that I do realize
It's you and I who've won

My Brain is a Jailer
James Hurst

I awake too early the silence is profound
The birds are not singing there isn't a sound
In the stillness and quiet I lie in my bed
But thoughts are like bees buzzing in my head
Jumbled and tumbled like a box of old toys
Swirling and flashing in a way that annoys
Be still my mind and calm yourself down
Ease off the tension and unwrinkle the frown
Leave me to sleep please be kind
Let me relax and let me unwind
But the brain is a jailer with no early release
It won't let you out and there is no peace
It's constantly working with no signs of letting
It keeps you up worrying and fretting
My mind is a battlefield it won't let me free
Is it the same for others? Or is it just me ?

Why Do I Wake?
Brendan Curran

Why do I wake on a frosty morn?
Why do I wake when I know you're gone?
Why do I wake in a lonely bed?
Why do I wake when I know that you're dead?

I wake to see a new day through
I wake to relive my memories of you
I wake to witness the good we have done
I wake to remember our happiness and fun

Waking is just the hardest part,
Waking allows you back in my heart
Waking unlocks the good you have done
Waking allows one more day in the sun

The Plan
Nadia Martelli

I plan to plan the perfect plan
So all the secrets come to light,
Before they scream, I scream, it seems,
And crawl beneath words that bite.
I know my "No!" cannot let go
Until its nuances are heard,
Until I deem the dream redeemed,
Until true answers are confirmed.
Now it's my turn to turn the key,
Unlocking more than just a door,
Releasing demons and their crew,
Blocking cause and unjust scores.
And I will learn and burn 'til free
Of nightly nightmares rendering me blind,
At peace, no reasons to bare anew
The mocking core of trust resigned.

All that Remains
Archie Papa

Brought from the arms of innocence
graced we may hold the reins
sought after dreams in the distance
until love is all that remains

Taking knowledge in footsteps
towards wisdom as it gains
forsaking fears along the path
until love is all that remains

Finding a way through the darkness
in whispers the spirit explains
binding the ties of remembrance
until love is all that remains

Shall Nature Be
Andy Reay

Shall nature be your dearest desire
To sit amongst a blanket of wildflowers
To absorb aromas sweet and warming
'tis the place to spend those precious hours

And pinkly fruit from wild trees grow
They glisten proudly in summer's showers
For your hunger and thirst be sated
As you sit amongst the wildflowers

From Absolute Zero
Peter Rivers

I went from zero to hero,
then back to zero all in one day
like a light switch went on
but just wouldn't stay

I burned my world Apocalypse
Now style in an instant,
to make something new in a blink

I flushed opportunity down the drain
to wash my hands of failure

I breathe a suffocating wind
for a chance to choke on calm cool air

I hack and I slash; wild, I throw fits;
I crash the calm for things to go smooth

I sweat streams of struggle to bathe
in a sea of sweet satisfaction

In that very same moment,
born within a panicked "NO"
A peace was found there laying on the ground
Sprouted from ignorance,
I bore this peculiar glow that continues to grow

This superhero will know how to put out the fire
when the flames are hot and the times seem dire…
There it is hidden inside of you, it's true,
a secret superhero only you can inspire…

Perseverance
James Hurst

Because I wear a mask and cloak with a hood
Because no-one cared and no-one understood
That I too have feelings that bring me down
So I walk through life as a fictional clown

Putting on faces I smile through my teeth
But nobody sees the sorrow beneath
I drive alone home and I sit in my chair
Watching tv with nobody there

Yes I'm a strong man, and yes I can cope
But what's life worth living if not without hope
So go to bed and brush my teeth
And bury the feelings deep beneath

So wake up tired but still alive
Get in my car and start to drive
To a job that has no meaning
Fed up now my eyes are streaming

If I could find another way
I'm fed up of this groundhog day
I've danced this dance and I've walked this floor
I believe that I deserve more

But yet I'll sit and take it on
My resolve not yet gone
For every day it starts the same
But yet my strength it does not wane

My Message
Richard Harvey

You may think my writing is dumb my friend
Cause I write about love again and again
Maybe you think that I'm not very smart
Cause my message is simple but I write from my heart

I just cannot help it. I want you to know
That somebody loves you wherever you go
Dumb I may be and not very smart
But I love you so much with all of my heart

So please take my message, though simple it be
And hold it in your heart, you have a part of me
And whenever you need it, as sometimes we do
Just remember my message, "I love you"

Tomorrow's Child
Mike Turner

When we look beyond tomorrow
And consider the world's fate
We may wonder where we're going
If we'll stop 'fore it's too late
Will humanity survive us?
Or vanish without a trace?
We may find our questions' answers
In a child's sweet, up-turned face
All the promise of our tomorrows
Is in a child's sweet, up-turned face

Yesterday's River
Mike Rose

Come later on tonight
I'm inflating that old raft
Gonna float down yesterday's river
Just drift away and laugh

I'm going back to the beginning
Not worried about the end
I'm looking for those golden memories
That are up around the bend

They come riding out of the mist
Glowing like a swarm of fireflies
Completely illuminating the night
They're a sight for my sore eyes

I watch them with wonder
As each one takes their turn
Trying to outdo the others
As their lights brightly burn

It takes me way back in time
I remember every single one
And it always leaves me smiling
Remembering the days when I was young

They say living in your past
Can be somewhat of a curse
But I always count my blessings
When I visit that beautiful universe

The Boys of Sorrow
Sinazo Zoe Ngxabani

I do not know what it is like to be a soldier
fighting in the eyes of glory
while looking into the face of sorrow
but, I know what it is like to be human.

I do not know what it is like to be in a warzone but,
I know what it is like to be a peace seeker.

I do not know what it is like to be anything
other than what I already am
and wanting not to be punished for it.

I do not know anything about anything
Or even everything about everything
But I know that this cannot be what is right;
I know what a scale looks like and this is pure imbalance.

Guns firing, bullets raining, everyone running.
Little time to pray, little time to live and all the time to die.
Falling and crawling on the dust
and bleeding to be in the arms of freedom.

The world preaches justice on high podiums
only to deliver its people to a table
of unjustifiable feasts of death
with world leaders hailing genocidal atrocities
and attacks, eating peas with a fork;

Invade, loot and conquer is their motto.
Propaganda machines work tirelessly
to bring manufactured news to poison our society's mind.
Manure, recycle bin waste, total bullshit is what I call it.

They sold their souls to cleanse ethnicities,
oppressing minorities with sickening atrocities
in blood contracts right before our very eyes.

World, peel your eyes!
We are the boys of sorrow shot right before our mother's eyes.
Somebody please stop the blood.

The Sorrow of Clouds
Tyrone M. Warren

Caught outside while scurrying to escape
from the torrential rain as if the police were in pursuit.
Rain so heavy & dense you can identify
the beauty within each individual droplet.
Let it be known that nature does not deceive.

Running towards that dry embrace
that the shopfronts exterior has to offer.
A brief respite from the sorrow of a cloud's grief.
Can you articulate your thoughts to others?
I ask this for the exchange of ideas
& the harmonious flow of information,
resulting in eliciting sympathy of the listener.

Your delusion is now in full bloom
as well as the field of shame that surrounds
& inhabits me.
Shame is a field, a vibrant radar,
to feel shame is indeed to create shame
because there is a certain part of me that
I would like to cover up
but in doing so the act within itself helps
& assists the shame to grow.

This is witnessed only by the Harvest Moon
which has been eavesdropping on my testimony
& the brief conversation between us,
but after all we're just mere
Carbon & desire!

Mandalas
Tanya Raval

Mandalas of life drawn out in sand,
Every circle, every corner balanced fourfold and fine,
The pain and joy, the despair
   and happiness connected with thine,
Love and sorrow all sung with the symphony of the band,

Every circle, every corner balanced fourfold and fine,
Life is still a mystery agonized by time,
The transient nature of sand art blown out as it's done,
To finish with life's lesson all washed out and undone,

Life is still a mystery agonized by time,
What was once there today be gone forever in mime,
Each curve, each space a sacred vessel of truth,
Body is just the vessel, the soul is the truth.
Mandalas of life drawn out in sand,
Love and sorrow all sung in the symphony of the band.

Priceless
Simon Drake

You drew me in unknowingly
Personality, an array of beautiful paints
Skin the perfect canvas to work on
Your zest for life, a multitude of ideas
Your warmth, gentle strokes of the brush
Your laughter, striking colours
Slowly piecing together a masterpiece
Your love slowly taking shape In front of my very eyes
Your sense of humour a beautiful unique frame
Encapsulating it all perfectly
You, unknowingly a priceless work of art

Everything and Nothing
Archie Papa

Everything to accumulate and nothing to achieve
with volumes of gospel and nothing to believe
time bearing moments labored to conceive
youth lays to waste what age will grieve

Everything to wonder but nothing in thought
so much offered yet nothing was brought
wisdom shares what knowledge sought
dreaming of peace as wars are fought

Paradise
A. E. Carey

The waves come breaking on the shore
And I could think of nothing more
Magnificent or beautiful
Crystal clear and most tranquil
Flowing over top my feet
This vast ocean in front of me
I step into the water's edge
The sky a brilliant orange and red
As sun sets clear out in the distance
In gratitude I'm here to witness
Sparkling water lays content
Reflections of the firmament
A piece of Heaven in my eyes
A miracle I can't deny

A Bond No One Can Break
Kirsty Howarth

I held you in my arms
For a little while
You weren't born alive
And I never saw your smile
We have a special bond
That no one can ever break
But you never had a chance
As you, the angels came to take
I'll never see you grow
And I'll never see you walk
I'll never hear your laughter
And I'll never hear you talk
I'll never hear you call me mum
And your first day at school I'll never see
I will always find it painful
That your life was not to be
I will always wonder
Who you would have been
I'll never ever see
You become a teen
I'll never have your first curl
Or even your first tooth
I'll never have your photographs
And I find it hard to face the truth
I'll never wipe your tears away
And I'll never hear you cry
My only memory that I have of you
Is of the day I said goodbye
Even though you had to go
As you, the angels came to take
I'll always be your mum
And we have a bond no one can break

Quickening Pulse of Lovely Things
Kate Cameron

Autumn quickens, tiaras of stars
flicker a frisson of chill
feet crush grass in shining mist mornings
owls call wildly in divine synergy
with a robust moon.

Under crisp falling leaves
my heart wanders lightly
with these swallows, on wires singing
condolences to those who do not migrate.

As soft as chamois are these warm winds
stroking the high reeds, moving on my skin
I am dew bleached, translucent
as these myriad stars, pestle ground.

A pulse of autonomy, the wine of the soul
I am changing my colours with the red-black rose
with the last calendula and its fiery glow.

Dark Waters
Kate Cameron

Oberon stalks this clouded night
the creek is lit in luminous light
as a dulled silver tray served to lovers

dark waters
absorbed in oyster beds
in small pipes of sanderlings
urgent feet and fluttering wings
stony root bound paths, a winding way
descending steeply

down past hoary pines
standing gods
dying slow
red barked myrtles
white flowers glow

cool waters
a pulse of flow
breaking hesitantly on the shore
bioluminescence of water
glittering against my skin
never known before
this light within

strange magic
give me more
of the wild woods
the dark waters
the other silver shore.

Awe
A. E. Carey

Waters flow right down to sea
I marvel in
Your majesty
Redwoods grow to touch the sky
To understand
I only try
Mountains reach the highest peak
The wonders here
Are what I seek
Clouds that rise and form the rain
Views that ease
All forms of pain

In this world that you made
A clear display
That faith won't fade
In awe I reach my hands to heaven
And thank you for
The grandest blessing

Spring's Derail
Karin J. Hobson

What is it in a movie that I see?
But, splayed out advancement;
A metamorphose akin to budding leaves
on growing gallant maturing tree;
Does not the season change,
like a rolling reel on theatre spiel?
A placid negotiating rearrange,
Derived by virtue's repeated range?

Is not a cinema scene a rebirth
of resurgence in a value's worth?
Does not a weary eye find pleasure
in the azure blue sky?
And, as spin comes to its final lap
with a flap, flap, flap of tail;
So too does Winter succumb
to the warmth of Summer's sun,
On the eve of Spring's derail.

Whispers of Yesterday, Echoes of Life
Lorna McLaren

The house creaks and groans, lets out a sigh,
dust motes on the air dance gaily by,
moonbeams cast shadows on empty walls
as whispers of yesterday creep round the halls.

My childhood home, now broken and spent,
as an ongoing memory I often frequent,
I'll sit by the window brushing my hair,
a reflection of life that is no longer there.

Nobody hears me as I silently weep
for what once was I can no longer keep,
while the world carries on oblivious to my plight,
no longer in focus, no longer in sight.

Forgotten to all, I have ceased exist,
yet in death as in life there is often a twist
as I hold the last card of the hand I've been dealt
so my presence around will forever be felt.

To the ones who betrayed me, you will feel my scorn
as each night, in your sleep, a new nightmare is born,
to all others that have shown me a kindness in life

I will bring you comfort in your times of strife.
Though I wander in time, alone and bereft,
knowing my life in your world nothing's left,
the essence of all that I used to be
will echo in the beyond of eternity.

Bedroom
Haytham Trueheart

I don't run anymore; I have freedom within my walls. Hours spent wrestling devils to paper, I liberate a kindergarten by the medicine in the pen. The evening breathes over my windows, the moon taps from outside, I rise and see creativity shoot across the blank canvas of night. Shrinking on the cusps of truths and lies, I float on the candles that enchant my inner muse. With an aptitude to sway through poetry, I have nothing to lose. With the rawness of poetry's sacredness, the highest price can never be bought. I am the poet, the flesh, the cosmos.

Heaving Breath
Imelda Zapata Garcia

Mi pecho late, al son de los cielos
Burbujas de sangre, ahogan mi llanto
Suelen fundir mi sueño y encantó
Y el lento latir, de mis desconsuelos

In heights that roam tenuous binds
Gasps of breath, escape my yearning
Engulfed in pining, thoughts discerning
Heaving heart of mine, solace finds

Entre murmuró de voz desesperada
Destacados prejuicios surgen relatando
La dulce verdad que viene despertando
En luz de vida, ardiente y desarmada

Bound towards alms, bequeathed endow
Preponderance of aspiring trust
Swells in bosom, with this, I must
Whisper hushed, my longing vow

Sleep Well Tonight
Valerie Dohren

Be still, O world, sleep well tonight
May all your dreams take gentle flight
Ascending heav'nly stairs sublime
Through all the corridors of time

To drift on lofty shimm'ring clouds
Enwrapped in bright celestial shrouds
Beyond the earth in regions fair
Without a thought, without a care

Upon a journey set in space
Another time, another place
Above the land, above the sea
There yet to find tranquillity

In magic worlds your mind to dwell
'Pon fantasies and dreams that tell
Of hopes, unmet, behind closed doors
And visions seen on distant shores

With pictures painted in the sky
Upon the wings of doves to fly
Illusions grand and heaven sent
Enchanting and magnificent

(Phantoms dance in shadowed places
Bright with luminescent faces
Floating through the mind, encaptured,
There with images enraptured)

Be still, O world, sleep well, sleep sound
May all your dreams with peace abound
Then waken softly with the dawn
To greet again a bright new morn'

Strangers Friends Lovers
Simon Drake

I just need to know it's over
This nightmare's at an end
I don't want to hear from you
Or speak to you again

Repeating perpetual cycles
Frustrating, arduous, annoying
Tables continually turning
With relentless finger pointing

Wreaking havoc and devastation
Looking back at what you'd done
You shot my heart full of holes
Then handed me the gun

Destroying the love I had for you
Twisting the dagger with a smile
Completely obliterating my confidence
Calculated and vile

Now I cannot face a mirror
Disgusted with what I see
An evil twisted spiteful man
Looking angrily back at me

Strangers to friends to lovers
I want us as strangers again
Eradicating you
from my memory permanently
I cannot wait to forget your name

Ghosts Define Us
D. L. Lang

I'm shadow boxing with ghosts,
doom scrolling down dead ends,
couch locked into lyrical loops,
a mind journeying spaces,
finding comfort in the chaos,
awaiting signals of serenity,
the danger is in the details,
evaluating realty's alternatives,
trying to crack the puzzle
of an image self-created
in a mirror that seeks perfection
within a world that isn't.

I feel a nostalgia for past selves
whose remnants haunt the landscape
near buildings long razed,
scrawled on records since trashed, and
organizations since disbanded.
Evidence that it was not just a dream
slips away with every passing second.

Friendly eyes and arms outstretched
remain etched inside my soul,
and though time and space do separate,
I wish only goodness for them all.

If I set foot on the shores of memory
will I reconnect to a part of me
that calls out in the night?
What wisdom lies beneath
the dust of returning?

What lies beneath the memories
that soften through the ages?
Is the answer to the mystery
buried somewhere in the breeze?

Of Silver
Andy Reay

Of silver that shines in the haze of sun
On cold winter's morning,
the day has begun
The trees, bejewelled
with crystals of ice,
gaze at this frozen world,
Awake from the night

I follow this landscape
through woods and shadows
Awakened sun easing through,
like arrows
This carpet upon the earth,
thick with vegetation
Creatures skuttle out,
does fire the imagination

I dream of worlds
with uniformed life
Rabbits as policemen,
calming struggles and strife
Dogs climbing ladders
and putting out fires
And a cat in the garage
changing your tyres

As daydreams dissolve,
I pull my coat tight
And crunch my way
through icy twigs, bright white
Through gaps in trees
the grey sky rumbles,
threats of a storm?
I take one last look,
and head for the warm

The Weeping Willow
Natalie Miller

In silence I lay by the weeping willow,
Caressed by the tendrils of her hair,
With the lush grass as my pillow,
She shields me from the sun's glare

An eternity I could spend here,
The clouds drift lazily across the sky,
The whispers of someone I love grow near,
It's as if we've never said goodbye

Her hand slips right through my fingers,
She calls just behind a curtain of leaves,
Her presence here, I know it lingers,
Perhaps my eyes she deceives

Through a maze of branches I grope,
My hands are wrinkled, and my pace has slowed,
I've survived years on glimpses and false hope,
But upon me her presence was never bestowed

Burdened with my grief,
The willow bends to hold me in her embrace,
Father time is the greatest thief,
For the world doesn't move at this pace

Opportune
Gregory Richard Barden

twilight ...

holds its breath
not for the sake of orbs ... or audience
that rare air, bestilled
holds quiet court in sole regard of
a mystery incomparable ...
there is a moment —
a wink of time
when the blushing cheek of sunset
plumbs its own depths
the smooth surface
ripening for a ripple of fancies ...
can you tell?
place your ear to the gloaming —
that hush hides a hope
and whispers of wondrous things ...
a mist of magic to spatter the
melting glow of dusk
soft-stained there, your lips,
parting ...
I am but your enchantment —
imp to your flame
and should I dare the embers, devouring
of my press upon yours
then it is a conjuring, carnal
of you ...
and ...

twilight.

Croaking Mind to Mind
Rafik Romdhani

An army of frogs croaking
mind to mind
Their voice, a sinister presage
of their near end.
An army of frogs where water
once was more than a friend.
But now it's gone after digging
Its grave with its own hand.
Singing out all night the spring
inside, these poor creatures
have nothing to wear
except the silk of the burning sun.
Only late night dew keeps company.
Each frog like an old car
wishing there were more.
An army of frogs at my own door.

Wind of Change
Lorna McLaren

Slowly blows the wind of change,
softly flowing, woeful, knowing,
clouds enshroud, trees are bowed
and sunsets are no longer glowing.
Peace will cease within the eye,
a storm now is a-brewing
drawing near, the atmosphere
all around is skewing.
As it begun the end has come
no time is left behind,
thoughts are raped, there's no escape
for we followed, oh so blind.

The Weeping Tree
Dale Parsons

Well, they call me the Weeping Willow
Yet I'm neither sad nor glum
The happiest tree, with billowing leaves
And I invite you all here with me
Well, they call me the Weeping Willow
Or maybe it's Salix to some
Here you'll feel snug, breathe a catkin drug
And relax in my pendula hug
Well, they call me the Weeping Willow
Yet I'm bright and like to have fun
Diminish in shade, I'll watch as you fade
Such joy to witness decay
Well, they call me the Weeping Willow
I'm wicked when all said and done
Kick off your boots, entice up new shoots
You're just fertiliser for roots
They call me the Weeping Willow

I Danced
Sean Timms

In spite of chaos shades and flings
Rapture and sweet rendezvous
Vigour gained from rigours faced
Life comes down to simple things
I've dared the devil and danced with death
I've dragged my chains
through times tight whirlwind
Become a prisoner of my past
Swore out loud and under my breath
mistakes blown away by
a transient wind of indifference
Over infinite fields of dreams I've danced

The Silhouette's Freedom
Donna Marie Smith

Against the darkening dusk, she cast off her silhouette,
An inky black contour set underneath the light of the sky.
A featureless outline now dancing beneath the moonset,
Cavorting and prancing into the night.
Twirling and spinning, performing a pirouette,
A desire to break free and liberate,
To forge her own memories that she would not forget,
To be released, unchained, to no longer comply,
Going it alone, with no contribution and no regret.

Death and Ego
Tanya Raval

He comes to me in the darkness of thoughts,
In the silence amidst noise,
In the angst of loneliness,
In the burning ache of wants,
In stormy nights when the skies are grey,
In the mirage of summer,
On dark unlit roads,
To show me the passage to the other side,
Where there will be no noise,
Just brilliant light and buoyancy,
A lightness and ease in the mind,
Peace in the heart for a life well lived,
And the soul all ready to embark on a new journey,
To merge with the cosmos.

The Yellow Road
Thomas B. Maxwell

There's an animal pack mentality
when violence erupts on the street
People record it, find it amusing;
entertainment to endlessly repeat

It's posted on social media
where people comment, debate and ridicule
The act abhorrent to those gentler souls
who see everyone's involvement as cruel

It's sad to see in this day and age
You'd think maturity would have prevailed
from a time when Neanderthal man existed
but that ship obviously hasn't yet sailed

A penchant for suffering, watching cruelty
or joining in when the odds are okay
Guaranteeing survival with little to no harm,
what's described as a cowardice way

Gangs are for unmanly, weak minded souls
who, individually, could thrive being good,
but in packs they're prey for the devil's intent
en route to Beelzebub's hood

the sower of seasons
D. A. Simpson

the sower of seasons
scatters seeds of autumn
across the realm entire

casting upon all
opulent colours of fall
in hues of gold and magenta
crimson and amber

sending a cool breeze
from the north
to ruffle the leaves of the trees
as they wither and perish

falling from their lofty boughs
and spinning to'ard the ground below
their final resting place to assume

until they are gathered to the earth
from seed to dust

while the quivering waters of a serene lake
lap at the deserted shoreline
in the pale light of early morn
issued from an invisible world

Your Arms and Mine
Brendan Curran

My arms are not your prison
they hold you to keep you safe,
My arms can only reach you
if you want my warm embrace,

My arms keep us together
on this long and rocky road,
My arms will always be there
to help and share your load,

Your arms have always held me
in a place that's warm and safe,
Your arms have always been there
when the wind was in my face,

Your arms are not strong arms
but they have never let me fall,
Your arms will always be there
when my back's against the wall,

My arms sometimes get shaky
when the fog and weakness abound,
Your arms still hold me tightly
they have never let me down,

My arms feel strong and steady
when I am by your side,
Our arms are stronger together
our love will not divide.

Antique
R. D. Fletcher

Staring at the tabletop,
Iridescent drops of light,
Images dance to music,
Muted in his sight.

Empty chairs and distant faces,
A hollow glass of beer,
He treads upon the memories,
The warmth that was a tear.

His life a darkened broken road,
A mind that's weak and worn,
Spirit challenged to the breaking point,
Since the day that he was born.

His fingers play the liquid stale,
As old and alone as he,
Musty smells, the tempest yells,
Lingers endlessly…

Unkempt and tattered are his clothes,
A beard so gnarled and grey,
They've been with him these empty years,
They'll keep him warm today.

Still the hopes and still the dreams,
And hold the pain at bay,
He lifts the glass unto his lips,
And the hours slip away…

I'll Take Any Crumbles
Jessica Ferreira Coury Magalhães

Could you spare a few words for my heart?
I'll take any crumbles
One morsel of your fondness
You may find it if you rummage
Deep inside your pockets
Along with love notes,
long forgotten
That you left there since you got them.

If you should find it your desire
To take one glance toward my side
You'll know that I could paint a whole night sky
Using one single drop of dye
Black — like the color of your eyes
I'll take any crumbles.

Along the Path
Archie Papa

All along the path of days
a past consumed, forgotten haze
we pay with attention, the abyss we gaze
the footsteps remembered on the path of days

All along the path of years
collecting laughter, shedding tears
employing knowledge, dismissing fears
the footsteps to wisdom on the path of years

All along the path of time
punishment fits our every crime
the future a riddle, the past a rhyme
the footsteps of life on the path of time

Sailing Cupid's Sting
Peter Rivers

I've got gills made for rapid shallow water
Would I taste the trident if I took your daughter?
They dine on puffer fish a delicate dish,
finished with tasty wine
I'd smite the lot of you, if it was the last thing I do,
our populace is in decline
I'm the Prince of Shoals the rocky surf my will controls
I come for the heart of the ocean, a jewel of a prize
A rare gift, to gaze upon her, and get lost in her eyes
She has vibrations and vibes unique, a silent siren's call
I can't explain it, she is my master
but hasn't mouthed a word at all…

Birdsong
Cypress Land

A stitch of stardust, a stretch in time
The quiet whispers, lovers sigh
Between the layers, lifetimes lost
My heart, the cost, my heart

It flickers here behind the eyes
As deep as Earth, as sure as Sky
In peripheral, a fleeting glance
A memory, by fate, by chance
Of you, My Love, in muse, in thought
An abstract sense, an ancient hush
A cosmic kiss full of promises
That isn't this, that can't be

Where are you now, in cloak, in gown
I feel you here, I call you out
In ink, in words, with verses roused
Where are you now, where are you

Poetry is My Way to Authenticity
Haytham Trueheart

Pulling my psychological flesh, a mind enmeshed. Poetry is my needle and thread. Splitting the insides of my soul, my ribcage letting go—there reveals a flag flown of autonomy displaying the mother of poetry. Within every atom pulsating from sunset and every impulse undulating from moonlight in my meaty cage, there children of poetry play and reside. Poetry is way to authenticity, a universal language of tranquillity. If one day, an accident occurs, and I am incapable of gripping a pen in-between my logic and emotion; pull the plug and drain all my melodious energy.

Childhood Jubilation Massacred
Brandon Adam Haven

Sprawled from 'neath the rigid soil of ire,
Belting a lyre of the world on fire.
Wailing ancient hymns of aged despite,
Stealing away the soft conscious light.
Sprouting forth disdain veiled by gentle eyes
Watching love die every time after time....
Spurned is the sky, weeping to flee,
Crashing aloud to an empty reprieve.
Gliding forth a warm thunderous wane,
Ascending through eternities of pain.
Gloating anew in hazen allure,
Dooming my vision of life obscured.
In fields of derision by a substance's blur.

These Steps
Anita Chechi

These steps are moving forward,
 now I cannot stop them
Whether you walk or not
 we will keep on moving

This is the sky,
 we are engrossed
Then why should
 we seek shelter?

We will keep flying
 in the sky like birds

These steps are moving forward,
 now I cannot stop them

What is the guarantee of life?
When will it leave behind
We will keep on living with love.

Passions of the Heart
Julie Loonat

Pen swirling
In the passions
Of the heart,
Igniting eternal fires
Of the soul.
 Erasing memories
Of traumas and travail.

Poetry elevates us
To realms higher,
Where we circle
On wings of luminosity,
Swirling the darkness
Of the void
Into translucent hues.

En Pointe
Annie Mitchell

She danced so gracefully, her violin waiting to be played.
Toe tips inside beautiful black worn out ballet shoes.
Arms curved around her torso,
Crouching white wings of a swan,
comforting a broken soul seeking cure before
death is bestowed upon.
Music gathering strength, no one plucking strings.
Sound swirls inside her head notes sing stories,
High octave voices accompanied each dancing step.
Reaching octaves, stretched,
No limits bound.
Beauty of form engulfed amidst emotions dying in sight.
Swan wings feathered soft spreading over fragility of life
Faithful to the end.
True love now freed from chains of fake identity.
Peacefully dancing a dying song bellowing
beneath the silence of breath.
Spirit takes flight powerless.
Leaving Earth purest empty
Shell lays still quiet.
Echo chambers begin to play
Louder than ever drama enfolding
with a forever farewell.

Beneath the Broken Skies
Steve Wheeler

Beneath the broken, bleeding skies
No fluid pathway shall be found
Out there, distilled upon the lurid streets
Beneath the broken, bleeding skies

Though washed and rinsed in livid hue
Soon will the sullen twilight call
To fade my colours into gloom of grey
Beneath the broken, bleeding skies

My pitched soul yearns the black of night
So I will stand to watch the dying sun
And sing a dirge to waste its final path
Beneath the broken, bleeding skies

Tomorrow
Bruce Stewart Hart

As darkness looks to brighten,
Is dawn upon its way?
Anticipation heightened..
But perhaps, too soon to say

Tomorrow is the gift,
That many won't receive
Tomorrow cast not hope adrift..
Nor deny me, to perceive

The sun has soon ascended,
And only time will see
Tomorrow remains pretended..
Assured of neither you, nor me

Mommy, Daddy, is there Something Wrong with Me?
Richard Harvey

Mommy, Daddy, is there something wrong with me?
Why do you fight so much and then yell at me
You send me to my room and then you close my door
Yelling and screaming, I cover my ears, huddled on the floor

Mommy, Daddy, I'll try my very best
To be good and not say a word, I'll clean up every mess
I know that you would love me if I could just be good
And then maybe our family could be the way it should

Mommy, Daddy, don't leave me all alone
It must have been something I did that is still to me unknown
Daddy slammed the door and left, Mommy's shedding tears
I'm sitting in the darkness shaking, my heart is full of fear

Mommy, Daddy, I wish I was never born
Maybe then our family wouldn't be so torn
If I could disappear and just stay out of sight
Maybe if I weren't here everything would be alright

Mommy, Daddy, is there something wrong with me?
I don't understand how I broke my family

My Soulmate the Herring Gull
Graeme Stokes

Good morning my herring gull
Are you feeling a little tender?
Or is it Miss or Mrs Herring gull?
As I can't ascertain your gender
Have you been banished, exiled, cast aside?
As you're looking slightly lost
Are you indulging in a bit of me time?
Some introspection from your flock
Are you on a spiritual odyssey?
Some answer to sustain your journey
If it's food you crave, then honestly
You should have flown in early!
As you shower me in sapient stares
Inquisitive head tilts
I sense a fledgling kinship rare
Mutual narratives to spill
Are you lonely in your coastal world?
Do you yearn to be a fish?
Do you have a seasick shanty to tell?
As you glide from ship to ship
I detect a most unlikely bond
A man and bird meeting of minds
Two black sheep in a scornful pod
Different, but on the same ride!
But alas I know, you have to go
For your home's the deep blue sky
But if our paths do cross, be sure to call
Fly forth and don't be shy!
You are beautiful my dear herring gull!
Proud beak and black tipped wings
And always remember that I told you so
As you soar to reach your dreams!

Ghost Town
Martha M. Miller

The swings in the park
move with an absent wind,
empty.
The sun, through the watching skeletons
of abandoned buildings
and the glowing haze of fog,
paints shadows of children
who once played here
on the ground,
like the echoes of laughter
now mimicked by the birds
with the scratching scurry
of the rats
through the detritus
of a newly ghosted town.

Zombie
R. D. Fletcher

In an era that's sick with selfies,
The narcissistic blight,
Blackened mirror called vanity's seer,
Its mesmerizing light.
In an era that's sick with frenzy,
The parasitic memes,
Image laced with alluring face,
Hypnotic zombie dreams.
In an era that's sick with cyber,
The apocalyptic night,
Empty souls in digit holes,
The screen that eats all sight.

Flock Of Words
Mike Rose

I was looking for a phrase
So I took a walk inside my mind
But after searching for a few hours
That thought was still too hard to find

I was getting tired of the darkness
When I spotted that neon exit sign
So I slipped out the back door
And stepped into the sunshine

I went down to the river
And stood quietly on the bank
Tried to remember what I was looking for
But only drew a complete blank

Then I walked through the woods
And climbed that small ridge
I ended up taking a seat
On the Skeleton Road bridge

The wind was howling
It was calling out my name
As the answer came roaring down those tracks
On a runaway ghost train

They had finally come home to roost
Like a flock of wild birds
And I felt like a proud parent
Holding all those precious words

Writing Brings Me Back
Natasha Browne

Do you ever notice?
That writing brings you to that place,
Where a memory is stored,
In your hemisphere,
Back to a place,
When you felt at lost,
Or inspired to write,
To ignite,
A flicker of a flame,
Not seeking fortune or fame,
Writing to keep sane,
Not sharing your work,
When nobody knew your name,
I came here,
Too write,
To shed some light,
On my many past grievances,
Harrowing deep into my core,
Where I always wanted somewhat more,
To explore the confines of my mind,
Shedding those underlying lines,
Where it was just me,
Writing poetry,
Not willing to share,
In the thought no one cared,
What I had to say,
Just me writing night and day,
Writing brings me back,
To that place I thought I lacked,
Something in between,
When my story was unseen,
In a place I'd never been,
Where my sane thoughts were intact,
writing brings me back.

Empathetic Souls
Melissa Davilio

empathetic souls know
the sunlight's golden glow
as well as the embrace
of the darkness just below,
how to bask in each ascent,
how to dwell within the shadows
of each descent's lament

Incubation
Martha M. Miller

The dragon snorts and rumbles in her sleep,
smoke sinuously streams from her nostrils,
ruby scales glisten stunningly in the low light.
She catches a scent... her sixth sense tripped,
and lazily opens one eye.
A gleaming glow fills the area with gold
pushing back the smoldering surly shadows.
Gazing through slitted reptilian lids to identify
the stranger, or invader, in her subterranean chamber,
the very heart of her beloved mountain.
She remains satisfied that she can subdue
any intrepid interlopers to her domain.
She gathers her eggs to her and snuggles back in,
listening to the tiny heartbeats most dear
as they tick tock like miniature clocks in her ears,
releases a sigh of sheer happiness and returns
to her dreams of days past...

The Quintessential Beauty
Brian Benton

Fibonacci sequence graphed on paper, pen and ink.
The beauty seen before me of which causes
   philosophers to think.

Mathematical wonders pass comprehension
   for you and I.
Making sense of life's puzzles makes me
   stop to wonder why.

Why is something so delicate, so rare, and so true?
Made so complex and so difficult to understand
   that which must have made you?

Moulded you from clay perfectly made
   from angel's tears.
Or slowly chipped from granite by bolts of lightning
   throughout all these years?

No creature I've seen on this planet
   we share here all alone
Compares to the perfection you exhibit,
   perfect symmetry, flesh and bone.

The most beautiful souls in heaven
   with their jealous torments made.
Make envy be their color and force their visions falter,
   memories fade.

The paint on canvas from masters
   in Renaissance time before.
Strokes from brushes no comparison,
   her beauty forever more.

The words lose all meaning, for description does not relate,
To the quintessential beauty, cannot turn away,
   attentions captivate.

What is a Poem?
Joan Audette

What is a poem but a star's whisper
A nod from the man-in-the-moon
Or a cottony cloud billowing proudly
Against the blue sky

What is a poem but the sweet song
Of birds in the quiet of the wood
Or the splash of a frog leaping
From his lily pad

What is a poem but the gentle breath
Of a babe at sleep
Or your heart brimming with love
Spilling out o'er the page

Paws for Effect
Sarah Sansbury

And just like that
we have a cat
he knows
he chose
he purrs
loose-furs
our floors
his claws
enjoy
destroy
our home
his throne
at his meow
we bow

Invisible Poet Girl
Jamie Willis

Today, I saw a glimmer
A little girl, barely four
Shared a cookie with her brother
crawling on the kitchen floor
She gave the boy the bigger half
Her angel eyes like sapphire skies
The simple joy of giving joy
when no one even knew or saw.

I saw. I saw it all.

We have a limerence with limelight,
Like it's the only light worth pursuing
The only things we recognize
are downstage states of daring doing
No one's beholden to the dark behind the way things seem
Like an agate overlooked in a peruse for pyrite's gleam.

There's a man that sits in solitude
At a library each day
His pen is scratching words on sheets
That seem a minds-eye repartee
I wonder who he thinks of
as he scribbles brilliant sheets
The greatest art is often made in quiet anonymity

Sometimes I feel invisible
I wonder if the place I have, the space I take,
my prism hues, the art I make
I wonder how much of this will be there to underestimate
While this rings of a dichotomy —
flickering flame, deleted scene
The dark is where the stars
always shine brightest even when unseen.

Cobweb Days
Sean Timms

You may cut me
  with your serrated eyes
  shoot me with your barbaric words
Just when you think you have me down
  in place
Once again I fly away
You may cover my soul with your cobwebs
As I gather the dawn in stone echoes
My song lilts on a gossamer labyrinth
  of moonlight hours
I think of us when our song
  penetrates my membranous labyrinth
We are each other's relief
  from a cacophony
  of tone deaf sycophants
Each other's equilibrium
I fell into a drowning pit
Torn clothes my dreams attire
Full of seething anger and remorseful regrets
In my darkest nightmare you saved me
  you pulled me closer
In your darkest day dream you learned
  that I'll be there to save you
  to pull you closer
I think of you in this aquarium dream
Laying there in a crumpled heap
Your aura reminds me of flowers
Once again

Cigarra
Imelda Zapata Garcia

Buried neath fodder for millennia,
deep under towers of steel
Covered by earthen gargantuan, interred
in a comatose drop
Burgeoning power of Angels,
wings of a chrysalis feel

Birthed from breath entombed,
risen from cerements, doomed

Slumbering hum of a whisper, hushed
in the still of the night
Cicada in mid of December, when icicles
seem to crop
Avowal of tomorrow to remember, below
nether regions of sight

Birthed from breath entombed,
risen from cerements, doomed

Dormant, this bevy of beauty, stuck there
collecting some dust
Aphonia, oh Monarch of longing, wishing
the watching could flop
Bound by impending of promise, aspires
a sweltering climb

Birthed from breath entombed,
risen from cerements, doomed

Do You Feel Me?
Graeme Stokes

I wish I was a dolphin, warm and snug in Cardigan bay!
An Albatross, gliding and rolling, absorbing all that I survey
I yearn to be a two toed sloth, just chillin' in the branches
A spiky hedgehog in the undergrowth,
on roads I'd take my chances!

I wish I was a crafty cat,
blagging more than forty winks
Aspirations of the common rat,
just to be a pest, methinks!

Be an alpha male stallion, the feisty fillies I'd give chase
Be a secretive rapscallion, a chameleon change of pace
I wish I was a humpback whale, the freedom of the sea
Do you dig the feast that I regale?
Comprende? Do you feel me?

I'd love to be a carpet, being massaged by warm feet
A much coveted egg omelette, to be whisked around lovingly!
The urge to be a village church, worshipped from base to steeple
An idyllic, peaceful grassy verge,
an arm's length away from people

A widescreen plasma TV set, and be the centre of attention
A monumental jumbo jet, then I'd really have an engine!
A cunningly placed revolving door,
and decide what souls can enter

Be the hands of time, that know the score,
a Swiss clock to depend on!
Be the cooling, laid back easy vibe, that is the summer breeze
Just to feel the jive, of a different ride, do you catch my drift?

Do you feel me?

There Are No Words
Kevin William McNelis

I wish that I could find
Some words as beautiful as you.
Then I could use those words
To write a song about you,
That I would sing every single day.
But...there are NO WORDS,
To describe you,
Or how you make me feel.
And...there is no melody
That I could ever play
To make our love more real.

Instead! When life is getting hard,
And I can't seem to find my way,
Or the boss is yelling at me,
Or I'm just having a bad day,
I'll just close my eyes,
And breathe in God's clean air
Until I see His radiant light
Reflecting in your hair,
And your amazing smile
Which I know is always there.
Then I'll see your green eyes
Pouring into mine
Until...I hear the melody of my beating heart,
And I'll know this much is true.

There simply are NO WORDS
As Beautiful as You!

This House
Lorna Caizley

This house we live, is built of more than stone
It has a special purpose of its own.
The roof above protects the heads below
Wooden floors allow little feet to grow.
Tall white windows illuminating gloom
of the strong walls dividing every room.
Doors that lock when the world needs kept at bay.
Open doors when you want to face the day
Cupboards filled with memories and clutter
A place to eat hard earned bread and butter.
A table to sit and put the world right
Curtains to cover the darkness of night.
Warmth of a fire to keep out the cold
A stable foundation lets us grow old.
This house we live, is built of more than stone.
Its special purpose is that it's our home

Yearning to Run
Linda Adelia Powers

The seas of the open fields are calling
I yearn to set my sails and run to my utmost
Until fulfilled I feel myself sweetly falling
The seas of the open fields are calling
Come rest in a peace finally enthralling
Leave all your worries, old fading ghosts
The seas of the open fields are calling
I yearn to set my sails and run to my utmost

Where Have You Gone?
Joan Audette

Where have you gone, my baby boy,
with your blonde curls and bright eyes?
No longer at Mama's breast…

You have grown
You have flown

Where have you gone, my dear young son,
standing so proudly on your first day of school?
Backpack on your back, new lunchbox in your hand…

You have grown
You have flown

Where have you gone my tall young man,
new whiskers now shaven, handsome in your tux?
Off to the prom, my teenage son…

You have grown
You have flown

Where have you gone my stalwart man,
standing so tall, proud soldier so brave?
Off to war, my baby boy, off to war…

You have grown
You have flown

Be safe
Be safe

Love Never Grows Old
Sheila Grenon

The echoing in brittle bones,
Love NEVER grows old.
Hearts stay pure as we endure,
Memories assure us as we mature.
Forever is the moment in our time,
As I write my next important line.
Reaching out as our love STILL shines,
no longer confined.
Sacred thoughts exult our souls,
Love never grows old.
Hearts in two ensues to glow,
Love in others we extol as we grow.
In one's own stale old mind,
We find newer ways to realign.
Love NEVER grows old,
Behold those who remain bold.

Flowers
Patti Woosley

F   Flowers in my garden, oh so
L   Lovely they thrive
O   Over the trellises, so
W   Wonderfully they climb
E   Exploding blooms of
R   Roses, reaching for the sky
S   Scents so heavenly,
      even the angels sigh

The First Leaf of Autumn
Paul Williams

Summers been dancing in gentle gusts,
The trees have had a rustling ball.
The birds have chirped incessantly,
They're so looking forward to autumn's fall.
Each tree, each branch are watching,
For the first leaf's smiling golden grin.
The spirit of seasonal autumn,
Is waiting for the first leaf to fall and spin.
The forest is waiting in anticipation,
Their golden colours and autumn show.
Squirrels, hedgehogs,
badgers and foxes,

Wait in anticipation under the canopy below.
Then a moment of autumnal beauty,
The first leaf to the tree says goodbye.
Golden russets of crisp wrinkled brown,
Slips gracefully from its branch up high.
It will swirl and twirl in silent fall,
Summer now takes its annual pause.
Waiting below a forest's animals,

In appreciation gives its seasonal applause.
Autumn will shed its coat of colours,
In the gusts of nature's breeze.
It will lay its carpet of golden brown,
And patiently wait for winter's freeze.

You Don't Belong To Me
Dashaun Snipes

"No!" I scream into the night
As I break the chains that held me tight
You don't belong to me
I can finally see
The truth behind your deceit
And I refuse to be your defeat
You don't belong to me
Even though you made me believe
That I couldn't live without you
But now I see, you were never true
Took me for granted, played with my heart
But I won't let you tear me apart
Look what you did to me
Left me broken, shattered and free
But I won't drown in your lies
I'll spread my wings and rise
No more falling at your feet
You underestimated my strength, my heat
You don't belong to me
I won't let your memories haunt me
I'll rise from the ashes, I'll stand tall
I'll be my own hero, I'll break down every wall
You can't contain me, I won't stay
I'll find my way, I'll make my own way
I think you lied to me
For so long, I couldn't see
But now I see through your disguise
I won't fall for your empty promises and lies
You tell me anything to keep me around
But I see the truth, I won't be bound
You don't belong to me
I'll say it again, so you can see
I'll shout it to the world, I'll let it be known
I won't be your puppet, I'll stand on my own
I've found my voice, I've found my strength

I won't let you break me, I'll go to any length
No! No more tears, no more pain
I'll break the cycle, I'll break the chain
You don't belong to me
And that's where you'll always be
In the past, in my memories
But I won't let them bring me to my knees
You don't belong to me
I've finally set myself free
From your toxic grasp, your selfish ways
I'll find happiness, I'll find better days
I don't need you to define me
I'll fly on my own, I'll be wild and free
Look what you did to me
But I won't let it define who I'll be
I'll rise above, I'll find my worth
I won't let you control me, I'll reclaim the earth
You don't belong to me
And I'll never belong to you, can't you see?
No! I won't let you bring me down
I'll wear my scars like a crown
They're a reminder of my strength
Of the battles I've fought at any length
I'll wear them with pride, I'll wear them loud
They won't bring me shame, they'll make me proud
You don't belong to me
I'll say it one last time, so you can see
I'll let you go, I'll let you be
You were never meant for me
I'll find love, I'll find someone true
But it won't be you, no, it won't be you
You don't belong to me
And I've finally set myself free
From your toxic grasp, your selfish ways
I'll find happiness, I'll find better days
You don't belong to me
And I'll never belong to you, can't you see?
So I'll say goodbye, I'll walk away

I'll start a new chapter, I'll find my own way
You don't belong to me
I'll say it again, so you can see
I'll find myself, I'll love again
And this time, it'll be real, it'll be my win.

At War with My Pen
Natasha Browne

I've lost the will to write,
Sometimes fight,
To recite in open mic,
To compete,
I feel defeat by the world around me,
The world within me,
The universe is in me,
But I cannot see,
Beyond the realms of poetry,
It's got a hold of me,
Won't let me go,
So, I'm safe in my word land,
Poetry understands,
It doesn't make demands,
Clutches my hand tighter,
Makes me a fighter,
Makes me feel lighter,
A whole lot brighter,
It is me,

Poetry,
You see.

Nam Hnub
Cypress Land

What came in transition of a Lunar wane
The rhythmic echo of an ancient chant
A cosmic fate of a Nova's edge
The atoms of an Adam never meant
A muted sheen, a silvery cast
Spot lighting shadows of an Earth in black
A wail, a cry, a howl unmatched
In defiance to silence the Sun

Opening Doors
Dale Parsons

One door closes, another door opens
But there's a hole there, deep and wide
Do you retreat through the door you came
Or take a leap towards the other side
What if that door slams firmly shut
It's locked and there is no return
And you stare into the void below
Where those flames, they bubble and burn
Do you smash down that door to go backwards
Or stay forever in the spot you are stood
Do you go forward, and over the flames
If you could pass safely, then of course…you would
For it is no easy task to move forward
But if you make the leap and you survive
No matter how hot the flames may get
You can open doors on the other side

Empty Shell
Brian Benton

Memories fleeting,
Visions fading.
Constant reminders from what was lost leave you
floating in a fog contemplating
the value of this life you're trading.

Lost in thought,
On the road to nowhere.
Travelling down a path
with no light forces emotions that make you bare.

Shining smile,
Regretful soul.
Hiding behind the mask you have created
so no one sees you have nowhere to go.

Full of ammunition,
Empty weapon.
Knowledge of the power inside you
but incapable of remembering death's lesson.

Lifetime of wisdom,
Empty shell.
This is why the enormous oak in your woods
made not a sound when it fell.

Audience all around,
Ears untuned to hear.
Shadows creep past the light you
once created until all you're left with is fear.

Darkest of thoughts,
Eyes full of joy.
Determined to keep going
and hoping all this you wonder will not destroy.

Let Me Sleep and Dream about England
Jessica Ferreira Coury Magalhães

I'll be holding a single red rose
but it will smell like Heaven itself
I will walk around my garden
And worry about nothing else.

A little house of red bricks
And a delicious pot of tea
No living creature shall disturb
This precious dream I'm living in.

I'll do the whole nine yards,
And I'll throw caution to the wind
I will put in more than three cubes
Of sugar — I want it sweet.

In real life, transportation is so costly
And you must pay for a flat in the city
But this is just my little dream
I live for free in my darling England.

I'll take a walk around the moors
And wonder about yore
But the trees, they have not changed
They'll tell the tales which men forgot.

If I ever leave my garden,
It will be to catch the train
To visit another town in England
And I'll be back, as right as rain.

Garbutt's Map
Iain Strachan

When I was nine, in nineteen sixty-seven
No computer games were found in schoolboy heaven
In those days imagination would suffice
Absent a flashing electronic device.
No laptop, internet, or smartphone app;
Our fun was Garbutt's Pocket Underground Map.
We'd unfold the grubby card and stare, ecstatic
Threefold delight revealed in classical schematic!
Multi-coloured lines denoting every track
Purple, blue, green, orange, yellow, brown, and black.

The hour-long trip from Northwood to London's heart
Upon the purple Metropolitan line, to start
Unfolded lovely poetry of station names that flowed
Like Pinner, Wembley Park, and Finchley Road
The high-backed seats on dusty silver trains
The memory of patterned moquette still remains.
Across the Finchley platform, changed to Bakerloo;
Its squat red forties cars propelled us through
The blackness of the tunnel underground
To Swiss Cottage, St. John's Wood, London bound.

But in the playground, with that map in hand
Far more complex itineraries were planned
To Ongar via the Hainault loop, we'd go
The changes all worked out, the route we'd know.
On the bottle-shaped yellow circle racing round
A few square inches, where adventure could be found.
Oh, the daring deeds we boys imagined there!
Dramatic rescues in our minds, from anywhere!
Although today bright high-res graphics are desired
In '67 a cardboard map was all that was required.

Frangere
Cypress Land

Lucent glow cerulean plasma
streams a-flow a-go between
diamond black the dust of old
and rusty clay red coral bole

Stole of Soul
as sands of gold
for bread and threads
in ruse she sold
mites and grains
of veins, in vain
for vanity's vain
by insanity's name
she claimed the Sane
as hers for game
as hers to gain
for pain is coin
to fare the toll
to roll heads up
the jagged knolls
of bluffs and fluff
to fool the fools
that tool the gems
that buff the jewels
that awe the muse
to muse, to bait
to sate conceit
to eat, to feast
to fill, to full
Ego's end game
Ego's end goals
as goes she goes
as goes we go
as goes it goes

but, you know

You know
You know
You know

The ways of ways
she plays her plays
her plays she plays
her ways

Control

Burden
Jyothi Bhagawat

Burden on the back
Accumulated through ages
Bends the body forward
Can't see the sky

Burden on the back
Physical and mental
Makes life unbearable
Better to think of remedy

Burden on the back
Pass on to next in line
Two better than one
Divide, make it light

Burden on the back
Let it slide own
Straighten the body
See the sun, moon and stars.

Frost Smoke
Martha M. Miller

In the valley that cradles
and gently manipulates
the autumn kissed Gasconade River,
a heavy white vapor hovers
in the diffuse light of early morning.
It's brushed with hints of pearl and pink
as blushing rays softly stroke the mist
exciting the night cooled air to distil.

My Truth's All Wrong
Nadia Martelli

Too long the tales of loss languishing,
And crimes committed against connections
That could have calmed all the chaos
And soothed the sting of sliced scars.
Still waiting for the weight of the world to wane,
Lest I suffocate beneath sordid sarcasms,
'Til the tick-tock of torrid and traumatic times
Subsides in the silky sorrow of its tune…
My truth's all wrong, fails at first, finishing
With rhymes unremitting in regret,
Misunderstood — too harmed, too tall the cost
Of being moved enough to sing to surprised stars.
Does hate store the Fate unfurled? Feigning
Its best lie, berated in morbidly dark chasms
That yet block the horrid and dramatic crimes?
I'll hide in the milky morrow of the moon..

Lines or Less
Ted Gistle

People always ask me
Why my poems are so short
I ain't writing nothing down
Might hold up in court

Messages of Madness
Peter Rivers

Desperately I've walked,
gasping and grasping
for satisfaction out of reach.
Why does tasting the sweet air held
firmly in my hands seem out of the question?
What messages of madness can I imagine
in this cup of noodles?
Oodles and oodles, bucket loads it seems,
all in the steam of this mug.
Wrinkled ripples shape the echoes
as I plunge in and out of memory.
Time slips and slides, these tender tendrils,
our celestial string things.
Becoming the suffocating weave
of our existence blocking;
feeling, reaching, then catching…
Finally empty I can see my reflection
in the spoon, it's me in a cocoon!

Reflections on the Shadows of Adversity
Neil Forsyth

As her days have sped past
and the decades unwound,
The mirror reflects
her adversities abound.

It shows in the lines
Of her furrowed brow,
The loss of so much
Never shown before now

Abandoned by her mother,
Left to fend for herself,
She never got to know her,
Got left on life's shelf.

Her inner turmoil raged on,
As her self doubts washed away,
Raised alone by herself,
Her insecurities allayed.

The passage of time seeped idly on by,
Her mum yet invisible,
Not a tear did she cry.

Then the raising of two kids,
After her partner left home,
A life she got used to,
A life spent alone.

But through all adversities,
Plainly shown on her face,
Her happiness could never,
without doubt be replaced.

She sought, it she found it
Without anyone's help,
Her kids, on reflection
Brought joy to herself.

Surrender
Susanne West

The Sea told me
to give Her my pain.

Trust took my hand
when I couldn't take Hers.
I gripped — and cried.

Together we poured
generations of grief
into the open heart
of the Mother Waves
until we were empty,
unburdened.

Lighter, brighter,
Trust and I bowed
to the unbounded devotion
of the Sacred Sea,
vowed to serve Her.

"If only the mourners knew
what was possible," said the Ocean.

Colouring the Wind
Jyothi Bhagawat

She drew the wind
And coloured it green
Since wind caused
Leaves and branches to move.

She drew the wind
And coloured it brown
Colour of earth and fallen leaves

She drew the wind
And coloured it blue
The curtains were blue
And blue sky peeped in.

She drew the wind
Coloured it yellow
The golden sunlight entered
And rays caused mottled pattern

She drew the wind
Coloured it black
Her curly hair fell on forehead
She blew at them with a whistle

She drew the wind
Coloured it pink
Wind blew on her cheek
And coloured it rosy pink.

Wind takes the colour
Of the things it caresses.

Wordslinger
Martin Attard

"Poet for hire," I'd confidently posted
"Unmatched rhyming skills," I'd arrogantly boasted
Certain that I was the best wordslinger in town
Each poem I fired off just increased my renown
I shot from the lip verses edgy and sharp
Blast off both barrels straight through your heart
I was top of my game, no one had a hope
But I strung myself up with my poetry rope.

The kid came to town, just like all the rest
Aiming to prove that he was the best.
He found me drinking in my favourite saloon
With a gut full of quatrains that made the gals swoon.
He was calling me out to a poetry standoff
He called me a chicken, then cautiously backed off.
I finished a sonnet then I slowly rose
Taking my writing-iron, I knew I couldn't lose.

The bright noon-day sun beat down on us both
Out triolet fingers knew the reckoning was close
We exchanged dirty limericks to warm ourselves up
Then he went for his guns, the insolent pup.
I rattled off Elegies, Epics and Epigrams
I winged him with Villanelle, Pantoum and Epitaphs
He stood there unmoved then began rapping free verse
He finished me with monostich then called me a hearse.

Poetry evolves — let's see what the future brings
The old styles are dead, for now — long live the king.

Red September
Jamie Willis

September heat is different
My roses gave up on reprieve
The petals falling languidly
Russet crunch beneath my feet.
Out of due time.
September's personality
is shades of borderline.
The summer's *pièce de la résistance*
Obsessed, and always wanting more
A love affair that ran its course
But leans shamelessly in autumn's door
Dry, but still oppressive
An embrace that lasts a bit too long
Awkwardly unwelcome
but determined still to linger on

The sky was red this morning
an eldritch dawning across my bed
The sailors heed this as a warning
Disturbances are just ahead...
My roses are no longer red
But faded to a pallor pink
The petals loose and scatter
in the arid breeze of ceaseless heat
The sunrise omen seems too late
Yet, I know the cycle toggles on
Autumn will not hesitate
To make its chilling presence known
But my summer roses have all flown
Nearly dead and almost gone.

I Want to Go
Jyothi Bhagawat

I want to go
Deep in to the sea
To pick conches and seashells
To decorate my
Chaotic mental space.

I want to go
Up on to mountain top
To pick few stars
Place them with fireflies
In a glass jar and watch.

I want to go
Round the earth with
Woollen thread to weave
A magic sweater for the moon

I want to go
Visit the stars and planets
Just to make contact with aliens,
and give my visiting card.

I want to go
Visit my best friend
To talk or listen to him
Drink or dream with him
One last time.

The Offering
Larry Bracey

I held my hand out toward you,
Offering you my bread,
Graciously you took it,
So your children could be fed,

You thanked me for the generosity,
Saying (you'd forever be in my debt),
My simple but kind gesture,
Turned into something you'd never forget,

You went and built a bakery,
Was it I who planted that seed,
Your debt to me was voided,
When you took care of those in need.

you are my oasis
Matthew Elmore

I draw water from your well
you know me so I need not tell
everything I have ever done
ever been or ever shall become
you wash me clean quench my thirst
leave only good take my worse
give me comfort from all doubt
so I can give my all when without
you shade my shadow illuminate light
early morning to late at night
you are the sun that my moon chases
when I am lost you are my oasis

The Origin
Michael Balner

I wish to reach out, touch the stars
I want to feel my fingers burn
The searing flame of endless love
One way trip only, no return

I want to fly and catch the wind
Singing atop of an old Lind tree
Then, I shall sing his song with him
Watch the leaves fall, and disappear

I need to scream and lose my mind
Float on a red wood timber raft
To where wild Nile once took my breath
And reminded me how weak I am

But when the sorrow floods my eyes
I will do nothing, I will not hide
I shall run through the fields of poppy
Into a dawn that leaves me blind

Yes, I shall tell you who I am
But first, let me walk the whole dark path
All the way back, to from where I came
The origin of a broken heart

Sturgeon Moon
Jamie Willis

Just ask a Cancer Rising
She'll tell you that the Moon's her friend...
The kind that keeps all secrets
The kind with which there's no pretend
The kind that knows
That beauty holds
Beholden eyes in captive prose
And bards who ballad bluest nights
That pierce like thorns of August rose
I rose to take my friend in view
Ten million Gazers did so, too
Awash in light of yesteryear's and morrow's
Universal Muse.

Rage
R. D. Fletcher

Rage, rage, against the fossil gods,
Cascading suffering and inconsolable despair,
Asphyxiate in their greed-storm fog,
This fragile Earth they ruthlessly tear.
In the heartless dark of our empty night,
Tragic Earth struggles to mend,
Rail against the dying light,
We plummet toward the planet's end.
Superstorms, contagion spread,
searing heat waves,
Ordain dark times and glacial winter,
Cry of extinction and coming death days,
Not with a wail but a whimper.

Children...
Linda Falter

Children are Nature's smile
They brighten the dark
And leave footprints
Across your heart ~

October Air
Joseph Gallagher

October air is angel's laughter,
Witch's whispers, capped from Winter's
First fresh, brisk breath
And seasoned with the scent
Of Summer's fruits...
What toot! What grandeur
In the final greens.

Reds like drum beats, banging, brawling
Like blood surge through capillaries,
As leaves unfurl, sap falling...
Crows caw-caw 'midst copper glints
Yellow, orange, tints of gold,
Stiff breezes hint at the coming cold.

Winds arise a rush and swirl
A whirling tempest in a tree top —
A mild maniac sonata surges
In a wheat rippled field.
Colors, gayer than any caballero
Clamour to the 'fore...
Fade, then yield —
Supple is the strength and glory.

The Reason I Come Home
Larry Bracey

If you're not from here,
It'll be hard to understand,
Things about these little towns,
All surrounded by farmland,

Its fields and open pastures,
Woods that go on for days,
Churches built by the congregation,
Where everyone goes and prays,

Swimming in the Salmon River,
Fishing a hidden stream,
Hiking trails and mountains,
Wondering if all of this is a dream,

It's about our friendships,
It's about our school pride,
It's about smelling the fresh air,
Each time you go outside,

I've been around the world,
And no matter where I roam,
I'm reminded of what's missing,
And that's the reason I come home.

Celestial Dance
Paula Rowlands

There is a celestial dance
between Sol (sun) and Luna (moon)
brief encounters with twists and twirls
to a harmonious heavenly tune.

Masculine and feminine energies
a balance of dark and light
living by the sun through day
Loving by the moon at night.

The sun is the essence that fuels
the moon the lineage of our soul
the sun dies away every night
so the moon can feel more whole

Occasionally they'd see each other
their love would tango in the sky
sun would shine, moon would glow
and then they'd say goodbye

Eclipses they do live for
a brief moment of such bliss
It's here that these two lovers
would always steal a kiss

Selene the Goddess of Moon
whispered to Helios God of Sun
though distance keeps us apart
'You'll always be the one'.

Between the Lines of Time
Linda Falter

Somewhere between the lines of time
People in our lives, come and go
It's not a question of why?
Maybe we will never know...

Daily creature comforts
Weave into our lives
Some we need and some
We hide...

Every new day is an open book
So take a walk around your life
And take a look, is it
The way you want it to look...
Some items we treasure
But is it a good measure
Our hearts know where
True worth lies...

Inside is a map
With twists and turns
And you never know
How close or far...
You are going to realize
Just who and where
You are, so face forward
And continue on...

Until your road map shows you gone
Between the lines of time

End of Day
Terry Bridges

A calmness extends...a vast level beach
No unexploded bombs to detonate my fury
This still evening beyond the tempest's reach
It soothes like a medicine ...no fuss no hurry

I tarry in the sweet afterglow of day
Linger among the rock-pools and ebbing tide
What is to come...a concern from yesterday
Forgotten in these nuances that abide

Detail upon detail drawn in the summer strand
I will remember each whisper of salt breeze
Worries collapse...washed away like castles of sand
The mighty empire of death brought to its knees

This triumph of arching rainbow over the sea
As twilight deepens and unfolds its canopy

From the Spectre of the Storm
Neil Forsyth

The sun reflected its dazzling rays
From the mists of early dawn
The day in its infancy opened
its welcoming arms once more

But change was already afoot
As clouds in earnest began to form
The rumblings of a rolling thunder
Echoed to a distant storm

The fiery prongs of lightning
Sparked across rain-filled clouds
As crowds fled from busy streets
To their safe and happy places

As the sky housed these elements
Busying itself with sorrow
The forgiving night streamed across
The sky with hope of a peaceful tomorrow

Butterfly
Michelle Tarbin

Emerging from her shell,
Like a butterfly shedding its chrysalis.
Creeping, crawling, pulling free from
the darkness that had encapsulated her.

Losing a friend had consumed her,
Eaten her up, entombed by misery and grief.
In the darkness she'd lost herself, sleeping.
Held in depression's cold, empty embrace.

Awakening from her slumber,
She saw glimmers of hope,
Light beyond the darkness,
Heard a child calling her name,
Smelled summer in the wind.

She rose, resplendent,
Her wings transforming her,
Let herself be carried upon the breeze,
To live amongst the flowers again.

Hoot Owl
Mike Rose

Late last night
When the stars began to shine
I headed down to the river
And decided to wet a line

I sat down on the bank
Barefoot in the grass
Then I forgot about fishing
After I made my first cast

I listened to the earth breathe
Then felt my spirit start to rise
As a south wind started blowing
Racing across those cloudless skies

I watched the lightning bugs glowing
Under that full moon's light
Then heard a train whistle blowing
Far away and out of sight

I had a conversation with a hoot owl
Who was high up in the tree
I felt that I could understand him
And that he could understand me

We talked about everything
All through the night
I felt like a much wiser man
In the early morning light

Dancing In The Dark
Kirsty Howarth

I keep on dancing by myself
Graceful and so slow
Dancing in the dark
So my tears will never show
A ballerina performing a pirouette
Being careful not to fall
Balancing on my tip toes
I stand so very tall
Dressed up like a princess
In the best and latest style
As I mask the pain within me
With the biggest, broadest smile
A polished, flawless dance routine
As the music fills the air
And to my attentive audience
My worries I don't share
Passion oozes from my pores
And my emotions run so very high
My body aches with every move
But for perfection I do try
I dance to tell a story
I dance to tell a tale
I dance to stay on track
As I try not to derail
My hair swept back from my face
In a sleek, tight ponytail
Striving for perfection
And terrified that I will fail
I keep on dancing all alone
While the light I try to spark
Exhausted and determined
I keep dancing in the dark

I apologize to my pillow
Matthew Elmore

I apologize to my pillow
for promises I can't keep
I even say I'm sorry
when I'm talking in my sleep
I'm sorry I neglect you
you're everything to me
I long to save the entire world
if only in my dreams

I apologize to the sunrise
of every waking day
that I may strive to realize
what differences may be made
communicating mercies
on which my heart do play
I reconcile every problem
that they all may go away

Shipwrecked
Ted Gistle

It's said "No man is an island"
Yet the waves on the shore speak of solitude
The gull cries echo with loneliness
And the signal fire is perpetually
extinguished by a tide of tears

Resurrected Poets
Gavin Prinsloo

Would you know if the Devil were Poe,
resurrected and born again?
Would that ravens call from beyond the wall,
that separates life from pain

Would Longfellow lay his head
upon the pillows of the dead, in houses plagued with ill?
Would Shakespeare shiver and upon a verse deliver,
words not of his will?

Would Plath defy eternal wrath toward those
who ended their own pain?
A thousand times writing the same screaming lines,
had she lived, would she do it again?

Would Annabelle speak and was Frost too weak,
to let death sunder loves grace?
Could she arise under death's cold eyes,
for him to gaze upon her face?

Could Yeats return within a Grecian Urn
to let a hand rub ashes desire?
Could Maya rise and her soul apprise;
would Mississippi still burn in righteous fire?

How would Neruda fair in the moon's cold glare,
if in despair he was awake?
What would Whitman sing,
what quote would Kipling bring,
if Heaven them both forsake?

I cannot speak for poet meek,
nor tell the story as if it were true,
Let them rise and the dead surmise,
what resurrected poets would do

Existence is Just Existential
David Catterton Grantz

Existence is just existential
You were expecting more?
That is all there is, my friend,
Said Peggy Lee to Salvador.
He fetched her jug of quintessential
And tipped her second pour.

You know that I'm not penitential,
No guilt, no shame, just as before
When we mingled like the wind
And no one kept the score.
But now our passion's deferential;
We both have learned to snore.

Growing old seems exponential,
A stubborn precept I'd ignore
If 'ere I could, and then defend
Vitality forevermore.
But existence is so unessential
And doors are only doors.

Yet life itself is not sequential,
Countered Salvador, and what's more,
On these glad wings we shall transcend
As we bend time around its core.
Though whimsy offers no credential,
Our laughter finds a fresh decor.

Save the Children
David Parazino

Save the Children now
They are the citizens of tomorrow.
They should be raised in love never sorrow.
They must prosper and never wallow.
We've got to save the Children now.

Every child deserves a future.
A future of their own.
Too many don't have their a real mother.
Being tolerated by some Other.
So many have been lied to.
Never knowing who they really are.
Family, ethnicity, and identity.
These are the keys in order to be free.

All the children have a right
To be nourished and nurtured.
And never be forced to have to fight.
To be educated in every way.
Protected from the exploits of strangers.
And dark evil days.

Save the Children now
They are the citizens of tomorrow.
They should be raised in love, never sorrow.
They must prosper and never wallow.
We've got to save the Children now.
Indeed, let us save the Children of the world.

In a Daydream
Nick Walker

The pastoral beach clad in silk
Oblong moons soft as buttermilk
Savory coconuts promenade my canopy
In searing suns I dream can this be?
Awakened by tropical painted birds
Their mystical song
Ablaze in a kaleidoscopic world I've pined for so long
One in nature, one in a moment's time
To be connected with all around is to be sublime
Traversing the cascading crooked rock life
Exploring all that is born
A shadow in the distance
I hear the fife
Melodies of tribal tune swoon my being
One-hundred mountains I climbed blind
Now I am seeing
Enchanted lands before me
I am lost and being found
Upon the moon's debut
Under its lantern I am sound
One in nature, one in a moment's time
To be as one is to be divine
I am shining in my dream
A luminous glow
Here I can fly in ways I did not know
Unbound, bindless flowing
with organic incandescent bliss
Fears sank miles deep
Some memories I do not miss
I know no time, no date, no year
In this fantasy I prosper
I cry not a tear
One in nature, one in a moment's time
Harmony lives in the air
The sun is my sign.

As the River Follows the Sea
Natalie Miller

O' lonely wolf,
Why do you cry to the stars?
When they are silent to your howls?
And indifferent to your scars?
The wind swallowed your song

O' hungry wolf,
Why do you put your nose to the ground?
For endless days, chasing bison
When sweet berries abound?
Your body broke on those horns

O' savage wolf,
Why do you sink your teeth
Into the throat of your brother?
Do you feel nothing at him writhing beneath?
Your kind is swiftly fading away

O' clever human,
The wolf said to me,
It is in my nature,
As the river follows the sea
And I could no sooner change the course

Not even you could turn that ship around,
Back to when the earth was new,
And change the laws to which we are bound,
Maybe you do not think they apply to your kind,
But all of nature shares one mind

I Am A Poem
Valerie Dohren

I am a poem —
I was birthed in solitude
in a place of quiet contemplation.
The words of which I am made
spilled out from my creator's pen
as a compulsion for expression and catharsis —
the birth pangs being both urgent and mindful.

I will oftentimes move your world,
perhaps causing you to weep or to sigh,
sometimes to evoke a smile or mirthfulness.
My greatest wish is that I should bring words of comfort
to those in need, a source of solace and understanding —
my purpose is cast within the cosmos
in which I was first conceived.

I existed as a separate entity from my creator, in fact
before there were any words
through which I might find expression,
for I am a child of the universe,
without beginning or end.
You may forget me, but I will always be here,
deep within your heart.
Take me, hold me, cradle me,
and treat me with the respect I deserve —
I came to fruition through love, care,
and dedication
and I will not be spurned or set aside.

I am a poem —
Sometimes I will manifest as grand and eloquent
whilst at others, I will be simple,
humble, perhaps lacking in verbosity —
but no matter, I emanate
from the heart and soul of my creator,

therefore I am a masterpiece,
a work of art, a thing of beauty,
and I must be treasured
and valued beyond measure.
Should you set me aside,
I will not be lost or disappear into obscurity —
I will wait, wait until once more
I find expression
through the voice of the cosmos.

I am a poem —
Open your book of verse

Read me!
Love me!

Love Letters in the Stars
Larry Bracey

By the way of Andromeda,
I've scoured the heavens for you.
The one and only true love
That I ever knew.

Banished to the darkness,
A prisoner of the night sky,
Constellations are love letters
Written between you and I.

As the seasons change
And when the nights are clear,
I remember that reading the stars,
Always brings you back here.

The Palace in the Valley
Nick Walker

The people had gone to their wars
Our motionless breadth
amidst harmonious perennial fantasies
The specters awash by the barrens
No wind could stir our chapel
An alluring angelic haunt amused
by Mother Nature's theater
Plush with silent smiles,
fragrant scents of caress and reverence
The trees faithful embrace sworn to our fidelity
No spot of ground in the universe and atoms to be —
Could banish relics and blossom the new
Ideals of solitude would arise to a quick end
Alas the pilgrimage ceased at first gaze
Entwined in regrets, mistakes, trials, joy,
and the present of now
The beaten menacing path traversed
To our palace in the valley
Where we'd lay our love to rest, to be.

The Tree
Darren Power

We met by the tree in the morning
with rising sun brushing strokes over the bay
seeing ocean's turquoise and diamonds reuniting
tasting salt air while watching pelicans at play
Your eyes met mine with a smile
with pressed lips breathing daylight anew
the beat of redemption with one love in my heart
blessed by three words never spoken so true

The Downs
Martin Attard

These hills of chalk surround me
Legacies of long-gone seas
This landscape could have drowned me
Yet my spirit is set free.

Tracks laid down in ages past
Wend through living history
Walked by people just like us
Passed from living memory.

These hills have run roots through me
Have bled into my poetry
Have shadowed and have sheltered me
With their open honesty.

I'll never travel far from here
I've taken them on-board inside
I'll ever call these hills my friends
Because together we are tied.

The chalk may crumble in my hand
The hidden flint is my anchor
She offers me her wild space
And in my heart I hold her.

I've walked these hills in every season
And in every weather
And though it's never quite the same
It also changes, never.

Treasure
Sarah Sansbury

Pay heed and admire
tenacity embodied
bare-faced beauty owned
carpeting fallow spaces
they covet our attention
dandelion clocks
marking time before the breeze
strong fragility
murmuring their soft language
of fine flowers of the field
what can it be like
this feathered-seed existence
once the Spirit-breath
with enveloping embrace
gavottes and grips and glides them
silver puffs of air
cupped in their Creator's hand becoming treasure
fruitful just because I Am
close-whispers to them, "You are"

Show Me The Light
Joseph Sawallisch

Show me the light,
for I've been sitting in the dark too long.
I don't know where to start;
one by one, when will it end?
I can't stop it, so I just avoid,
hoping that one day it will all be gone —
forever with me, it will be done.
I refuse to quit and let this win,
but that doesn't mean I'll let you back in.
It simply means I need to start over again.

Shadows
Sarah Wheatley

As two ships do pass at night
And eyes do seek the sun
The sailors hearts a-filled with fright
At beasts may be to come

So too our minds are raged with monsters
Rising from the depths
Tormented, dark waves rise, crash, curve
Hide the unhappened yet.

For beasts are formed of many shapes
And most are the unseen
We shy behind protective gates
Forgetting how to scream

But like the depths, the sailors' haunts
Soon true shadows appear
Think this when you have lost the shallows
And drown yourself in fear

For the noises that grow from our souls
Are often made of self
And when we let the beast dissolve
We find, our mental health

Moon Song
Gregory Richard Barden

there flames a fire in the sky
    it burns, though pale and waning
        my somber heart and griefs depart
    midst heaven's weep, now raining …

    ~ oh moon, you pull no tide
        as deep as what's inside ~

there spins a flicker in the dark
    that trembles bright, should fashion
        one dreamt escape with curving nape
    back roads that wind to passion …

    ~ oh moon, you paint no skin
        more charmed than that I'm in ~

there pouts a glow in even's arc
    that whispers through the heather
        and sings to death in twilight breath
    sweet hopes for morning's weather …

    ~ oh moon, there are no dreams
        not drenched amid your beams ~

there shimmers gold within the ink
    her moonlight eyes — cool-blazing
        it pulls me deep down to their keep
    the depths I've drowned, a-gazing …

    ~ oh moon, there is no fur
        as soft as you … on her ~

how you both make me stir.

Beach Glass In My Hand
Neal Klein

Loss,
like beach glass,
freshly broken, it cuts, razor sharp.
With age, over time,
the glass, a piece of the whole,
still pulls on strings that play my heart.
Filed by elements —
water, sun, wind blowing sand —
weathered glass, buffered and dull,
lies cradled, heart in my lonely hand.
Its muted color deeply cherished,
smooth, soft, tactile texture gently held,
as I rub my thumb
along time-worn, rounded edges,
love's memories, deeply felt.

Enter
Susanne West

Enter
the eyes
of the shunned ones
that lead
to the Heart
that leads
to the Infinite
that dissolves
all the names
that made us two
that remember us now
as One

Love
Wayne Riley

She has given me
The best years of her life.
And I have given her
The worst of mine.
The monster that
Haunts my soul—
Haunts hers too.

And for that
I expect no forgiveness.
The death of her smile
Is more pitiful to see
Than the loneliness
In an empty room.

Only the outline remains
On her face—
Stained into the lines
Like a faint memory
From a distant life.
Yet the search for hope
Goes on—
Denying the sadness
In her heart
The chance of freedom.

How cruel the burden
Of love can be
To a rose
Deprived of its wings.

Bleed
Byron Hawkinson

Silenced, with breath held tight.
In solitude, you suffer the night.
Never again shall you breathe—
In shadows beckoning reprieve,
I want to slice you and see you bleed.
Now you linger, an apparition of the past,
Haunting my every thought,
My sorrowful wishes unspoken,
Entwined to a dark night's demon awoken.
Here, there is no longer you and I,
Just echoes of what we once were…
Seeking absolution to recede,
The dark billow within your empty dreams,
Your suffering so vast and unrelenting,
The corridors of emptiness repenting.
Thus, let the darkness consume you,
Forever you bathe in gravely bloom.

Lavender Lullabies
Melissa Davilio

Lavender lullabies
flutter like butterflies,
whispering upon the breeze
outside my window,
where I'm propped upon a pillow
listening to the sea,
the waves singing gently to me,
as I close my eyes,
drifting away,
letting them lull me to sleep.

Great Waste
Joseph Andrew Miller

A gust of hot wind
Beats angrily
Against the placid sea
The skin of a drum
That undulates
Growing under multitudes
As more strange winds mix foes
A ripple into raging tides
Great squall
A tidal scythe to cleave away
At least a single tree
That distant gust once destined
As a breeze upon that tree
A breath to fill a blossom
That would have sailed
Across the sea

Snow Snakes
Matthew Burgio

A drifting blur of ghostly white
That's carried by a gentle breeze.
They scurry on as if by fright,
And disappear with knowing ease.

My car it cannot seem to seize
These creatures crawling 'cross the street.
Avoiding that which can't be beat,
They slither off into the trees.

They disappear with knowing ease,
And scurry on as if by fright.
All carried by a gentle breeze,
A drifting blur of ghostly white.

Waterborne
Corey Reynolds

water is what I need
I see it pour I watch it cascade
rivers and streams flow to and from
this ocean of my youth and of my dreams
water contains all the drops of my heart
beating away as time evaporates and returns
individual and unique in its misty spray
travelling through poison and darkness
 open daylight and clouds of itself
taking turns leaving me and returning
reborn as an ocean blue to my adoring senses
 keeping me alive inside
I remember it well

The Speed of Sound
Paul Welsh

At seven hundred and sixty seven miles per hour,
You're breaking Mach one with impossible power,
when the vapour cone peaks with unimaginable grace,
you're lightening on fire at an inconceivable pace,
a sonic boom burst like you've never heard,
you're a blast from the past that the present declared,
as the onlookers gaze with a jaw dropping gape,
at your superman guise while you're wearing a cape,
as your velocity climbs and your celerity breaks,
the atmosphere bounds you're a bullet in haste,
then you reach for the sun and all the matter that's due,
is you're a shot from a gun as you move to Mach two,
the heavens take heed at your expeditious intent,
as your marvelling speed at a million percent,
everything you regard and all that you see,
is within your grasp as you move to Mach three.

Garlands
Ryan Morgan

When the magnolias fall
He'll be gone.
Their swift fragrance
As incense garlanding
His padding passage.
Delicate with dewy nectar,
Attar wept over life's altar
At the terrible wonder
Of brevity's bloom
That must shrivel then sink,
Often graceful,
Other times roughly shaken,
Yet always the fall of all
Fated as the season's turn.
The blossoms drift like his years.
Gentle, abundant,
A patternless petal scatter
Of alabaster curls
Fading, feeding back
Into the sacred soil.
As they become one
With the fortunate Earth

Of Course
Ted Gistle

People ask if I'm okay
Of course I am, I'm flying
Ask if I'll stay another day
Of course I will, I'm crying

The Eyes of a Bridge that Sleeps
Donna Marie Smith

Take a trip underneath its arches,
Through the eyes of the bridge that sleeps.
Float down amongst its waters,
That meanders far and deep.

Sail within its vision,
Explore all that's captured in its dreams.
Traverse in the sights it cannot take,
As you sail amongst its streams.

Behold the wonders that it holds,
That it conjures in its mind.
As you take a stroll along its path,
As it weaves and intertwines.

Experience all that it cannot,
Down its paths that flow and sweep.
Take a trip underneath the arches,
Through the eyes of the bridge that sleeps.

Mesmerizing
Nan DeNoyer

Music, it set the rhythm,
tempo ignited their soul
into a burning flame
it consumed them beyond
into another dimension.

It drew them to embrace
its mesmerizing movement
capturing the soul

into their web of disguise
desire with no return.

Intriguing the beat
Tantalizing it was, as
they danced entwined
magical was the moment
they transcended time and space.

Greyhound
Michelle Tarbin

Those soft brown eyes have seen a lot,
He came to us broken and scared,
A former racing greyhound with a broken tail
and tattooed, crinkled ears.

A long, lean, slender body,
Stretched out and facing away,
The anticipation of rejection, again,
Another black greyhound, they would say.

His paw wouldn't leave my hand,
On that long, smelly, car journey home.
He'd lived at the Dogs Trust for eight months,
No interest had been shown.

Watchful eyes observed me,
He cried when we left the room,
The bemusement when the television was turned on,
He'd not lived in a house before.

A forever home was needed,
For this anxious and weary soul,
We taught him how to play and trust,
And then he stole our hearts.

The Essential Stitch
Ryan Morgan

Connection is the natural
State of reality.
Nothing exists alone.
Every object in the universe
Is in a relationship of gravity
And holds together
Everything else.
Every movement effects
The motion of the whole.
Even solitary stillness
Is an illusion of isolation,
As the seemingly static
Shuttles through time and space
Whilst others orbit and oscillate
Around their sequestered place.
Nothing is isolated
Or can be alone.
All matter matters.
We all are threaded together
In linking lines.
Each person is a part
Of the woven whole.
All acts and omissions,
Decisions and vacillations
Affecting the fabric of forever,
Warping and wefting one another,
Into the composite cloths of creation.
This fact of our existence
Is indelibly dyed
Upon the tapestry of the universe.
Every one of us
Is both cause and effect,
Changing all that there is
Just by being.

Inflating Life
Jodeci Flores

Breathe in, breathe out,
the babe afloat, just chillin';
free limbs extend, explore their reach,
yet bound by space, still giving.

Inflate the red ball beach —
pulls the air out of me;
makes it blurry,
lungs tired, taken by siege.

A wailing swan dive before the scurry,
into the world, born of splash,
the water carries me on — no worries,
my kids in the pool, whiplash.

Marco and Polo on a mission,
let's laugh and play, free jurisdiction;
red ball's expansion, afternoon in action.

Soul Cleansing
Phillip Burgio

Every so often I will cleanse my soul
Of grief and sorrow and other woes.
I do this by music that reminds me of her
And other thoughts that I hold dear.
I let the sorrow escape down my cheek
The relief from sorrow that I seek.
It takes the burden off my chest
And gives me some much-needed rest.
The grief and sorrow will creep back in,
But I won't let the sad thoughts win.

When The Night is Empty
Martin Attard

When the night is empty
The stars are curtained off
No sounds from the highway
I hesitate to cough.
Critters hiding silently
In the heavy rough
When the night is empty
The silence is enough.

I took a walk along the street
In streetlight blur and shadows
I felt the stillness of the night
The hush upon the meadows
The only walker in the world
The only serene wanderer
Senses straining fruitlessly
A solitary night ponderer
I felt the absence of the waves
That normally crash endlessly
I felt I'd reached a turning point
Received a message soundlessly.
A premise that if followed through
And brought to crystal clarity
Was shattered by approaching cars
and returned reality.

When the night is empty
And you embrace the emptiness
The universe can disappear
and lucidity can coalesce.

The Strange Sympathy of Pendulums and Fireflies
Joseph Gallagher

Someone in the sixteenth century,
A maker of metronomes
A patron of pendulums,
Observed the constant consonance of clocks
Enclosed in glass boxes...
Even those with inconsistent cadences
Eventually marched in steps of lock.

In the same way discordant metronomes
Became synchronized,
The fireflies of Southeast Asia
And the Smoky Mountains drape
Their ethereal landscapes like jewelled crepe
In a cohesive luminous dance of light and dark.

The firefly's undulating spark
Is susceptible to lithium bulbs and neon lights,
Buzzing cities transistors turned to stark
Bristled brightness. Fireflies become
Daylight moons to too many suns.
Their mating dance is fading before it's begun.

She and he neither buzz nor sing
For mates whose hopes include no rings.
Only a pale green fire encased
In translucent gold...
Shaken like morse code maracas,
An erotic effulgence desire unmatched — Behold!

Now the electric fizz of cobalt glass
Whose glare obscures...
Drowns their synonymous love
In unquiet pools of light.

Once our species wandered by dirt lanes
In pitch dark, led astray by flowers, spells,
Fairies, sprites and ancient elves...
To seek what daylights cloudless skies
Hid from humdrum human eyes,
Now sought to succumb to stranger selves
Where love and danger in equal measure hide
And fate or destiny is not yours to decide.

Now though the utter dark is dissolved
And desire, fireflies and clocks are out of sync,
Chance and mystery too have all been solved
Once we were chains in an ancient link...
Now we are codified, calculated, clinical, evolved,
We stand calcified, critical, on the edge of the brink.

I think some things can only be found lost
In the dark,
Somewhere far beyond the light
And oh my love, my love—
I am hiding here in plain sight...
Hiding from the dawn,
That is nearly now upon us.

Mind Set
Nicholas S. Leslie

In my mind you will see
That there is a better
Part of me for I was given
A shell of a corpse only to dwell
Along the floor as I lay
I start to stray I creep and crawl
Toward the fall Into the hole of agony
Then I hear laughter and wonder

if it's from fear I'm sure they mock me
I am aware but my mind is sharp
So as I build my courage to hold
Onto my thoughts around me
Inside my mind is the place I thrive
Nothing can contain me
My fears have grown
Stronger than I know but what is fear
When I have hope for I have tools
I am no fool to bury loads of burdens
As weights are lifted
I rise as if I were gifted
I rise from the floor
I shall not be a corpse
No more I was always meant to soar

Embodied
Neal Klein

My dog Harmony ate my poem of grief.
Maybe she has good taste.
I didn't think the poem was that good either.
But as she rests on the floor next to my feet
and looks up at me,
her eyes seem sad, and
I wonder if, instead of being critical,
she wanted to swallow my sadness, so
I lay down beside her,
to feel her chest rise and fall,
hear and smell her not so sweet breath,
listen to her heart,
feel my cheek on her wavy coat of soft wheaten fur,
and love all the love she has left

Warm Mangroves
James Garrels

Ocean sea, I breathe beneath thee so discreetly.
Amongst the waves, I may be seen as they sweep away sweetly.
They put my grasp to the test as I hide in my ocean grass.
I breathe my last, and I pass.
Now, in the warm mangroves, things don't move fast,
and here I am at last.
Because of my mighty grasp, I passed the ocean test.
So I don't miss the ocean grass where I take my last breath.
Warm mangroves, I have come at last.

It Takes Two to Tango
Melissa Davilio

While last ditch efforts
may be met with failure and regrets,
you can place that safe bet
by upping the ante,
the rewards can be plenty,
when if you don't take that chance
there's no hope for romance,
and the gesture need not be fancy,
nor of an extravagant cost,
and simply the toss
of a downfield final Hail Mary pass
can yield good results, as it shows
you're willing to learn how to dance,
to go with the flow,
to reach your end goal,
as we all know,
it takes two to tango
through the rhythm of life,
or better yet,
to perfect the flamenco.

Colors Within
Hannah Gray

The world still hums beneath her hands,
A language whispered through the sands.
Though darkness wraps her like a veil,
She feels the earth, the wind, the sail.

Once, she danced with skies of blue,
And bathed in dawn's most golden hue.
Her eyes once kissed the stars at night,
Now they rest in quiet flight.

Yet memory keeps the colors bright —
The crimson leaf, the pale moonlight.
She knows the sun, though out of sight,
Still warms the earth, still burns with might.

Her heart can trace the violet hills,
The rivers' song, the gentle thrills
Of flowers blooming in the breeze,
Of endless worlds she still believes.

Though sight has fled, she cannot mourn,
For in her soul, the world's reborn.
And when the stars rise high above,
She knows their dance, she feels their love.

For in her dreams, the colors stay,
In lightless night or brightest day.
And though the world is dark and wide,
Its beauty lives inside her mind.

Rebirth
Sarah Wheatley

The depths of slumber
Wake the soul
To images of Ernest

We count the number
Til dissolve
Our minds into the furnace

To burn away
The outer cloth
That shrouds our inner thoughts

We linger there
Til soon we're lost
And in our darkness caught

Yet soon we rise
And up within
We see a clearer state

The true alive
Felt in our skin
Allows negotiate

Our so we leave
The darkness there
And move towards a light

To shed torn sleeves
And soul repair
By sleep that comes at night.

Color of My Soul
Rose Marie Streeter

My heart weeps as
darkness overtakes me
colors my soul
in shades of black...
my being crumbles
into hole of abyss
where demons echo
their chants of doom...
still...
I look toward the heavens
knowing peace will be mine...
as new harvest moon
colors my soul...

War in Pieces
Neal Klein

A child recounted,
in a tremorous voice,
a thousand visions
he cannot unsee.
"We were baking bread.
We were breaking bread.
We came to blood,
and martyrs scattered.
We're gathering them in body parts,
in body parts and pieces —
The civil defence members came,
and gathered them,
gathered them in pieces,
as if anything mattered
My friend died.

They also picked him up,
picked him up in pieces.
Everything—everything,
everything is in pieces. Everything,
is shattered.
I want to live in peace,
in peace,
not, in pieces."

Abundance
Lana Martin

I'm looking at you again
in abundance of morning dreams
peeking beyond the horizon
running their fingers through my hair...
although awake
with closed eyes I feel and see
your peace in the play of light
blissful touch that opens my eyes
painting your love with birdsongs.
I love you and I wake up every morning
with closed eyes
so they don't see you
so they don't take you away
in the simplicity of their thoughts
on an ordinary morning for those
whose shackles of superficiality on their hands
tie their minds with blindness.
and I love you with closed eyes
while you dress me with dreams
in an evening dress
for love tailored
for much more
even more than this morning.

As You Are
Michael Balner

When the heavens open wide,
And the stardust rains on you
Like dandelion seeds that fly
On a mellow summer afternoon;

And when it shines in your black hair
Like sunlit mountain river ice,
so bright that it hurts — so badly,
Know that I won't close my eyes.

When the flames of a searing fire
Spring up from your aching heart,
And the wars raging inside you
Flood your senses, and you cry;

When they blossom on your lips,
When your pain tears me apart
Into a thousand bleeding bits,
Know that I won't close my eyes.

I may blink, and I may squint,
But I shall never close them,
I shall see you shining bright,
I shall see your bleeding heart;
I shall see you as you are.

The Sea
Kirsty Howarth

Dangerous and wild
Calming and serene
Unpredictable and inviting

Distant and pristine
Welcoming and quiet
Angry and uncontrolled
Turbulent and tempestuous
Beautiful and cold
Deep and also shallow
Shimmering with light
Sharp and sensuous
A hypnotising sight
Powerful and raging
Habitants unseen
Stormy and rough
With shades of blue and green
Demanding and dramatic
Treacherous and strong
Radiant and tranquil
Wide, bottomless and long
Troubled and hungry
Urgent and unknown
Limitless and cruel
Rapid and alone
Exotic and timeless
Endless and un-hushed
Immortal and refreshing
Impatient and unrushed
Spacious and sacred
Mysterious and pure
Ancient and eternal
Dazzling allure
Transparent and chaotic
Violent and confused
Bitter and naked
Fearless and abused
Flawless and unattended
Polite and also rude
Boisterous and savage
Easily misunderstood
Loud and open

Refreshing and old
Glorious and gracious
Bashful and bold
Remarkable and uncertain
Tireless and vast
Deceitful and sun-kissed
The future and past
Restless and vicious
Emotional and immense
Sleepy and alive
Extreme and intense
Victorious and doomed
Urgent and free
An expanse of water
That is the sea

Folds of Time
Andy Reay

We wander through the folds of time
Temporal nomads, we flit back and forth,
witnessing all manner of marvels and horrors
We pass through corridors, doors unlabelled
Each one a surprise, adventures new

We appear as ghosts, observers sometimes seen,
oftentimes ignored
Some favour a moment, and stay there,
wandering through stately homes,
or observing the world through windows

We are though living beings, transparent in nature
We have lived and loved, but crave adventure
New stories learnt, new songs to sing
We are temporal nomads
Wanderers through the folds of time

The Maker's Memoir
Jodeci Flores

Rustle, tussle,
Everything's a bustle,
all together,
nothing, nowhere, forever.

Unfolding, remolding,
insides are unrolling,
what a vast space —
just I, full of grace.

Lonely, all-knowing,
teachings, bestowing,
may consider exploding,
a billion pieces, I can guide.

Cha-cha slide,
worlds collide,
screams of victory,
as my sorrow subsides.

But wait — hold on,
my children are calling,
their joys in the distance,
so real, so enthralling.
...

I'll finish this later —
I'll be back.

34 Kisses
Lana Martin

thirty fourth kiss
resting on my lips
after sixteen pages
my heart engages
in the lethargic flight
beautiful and bright
within visions of your paradise
twenty first was a surprise
on page thirteen
when I was a teen
with no one around
to our faith bound
twenty one kisses
my soul misses
the land of free
under a family tree
where river flows
while bloody wind blows
thirty four break ups
in broken tea cups
tea made of petals of roses
delivered in small doses
to our childhood end
sinking into the sand
of twenty one beaches
where life teaches
lessons not learned in school
meant only to fool...
to uprise thirty four hopes
for my soul with yours elopes
leaving forty kisses for later
tipping an invisible waiter
in a cafe where they sell pain
and board children with a crane
transporting reasons

distorting seasons
for thirty fourth kiss
resting on your lips
when we were forgotten
in the fields of cotton...

The Tangerine Dream
Paul Welsh

When the dazzling bright etches
the silhouette of the hillside,
and the sun dons the clouds like a crown,
as the shadows of waves linear track the horizon,
then I'll know I've been lost and been found,
the firmament glows in a tangerine dream,
and tans the wisps of the clouds overhead,
the shadows of waves linear track the horizon,
as the sun dons a halo of red,
that's when I'll be home, the solitude lost,
no longer beached on the coarse sands of time,
when the bright yellow orb mellows the cost,
of the days that are lost in a rhyme,
that is when you'll see me apparent appearing,
cloaked in a vista of dusk,
with the sun hypnotised
by a man with a meaning,
no longer impatient and brusque.

A Poet Made In December
Jou Wilder

Last December night, in the dull ember light
I wrote my first poem to you.
Fragmented lines and disjointed rhymes;
I only capture the stress on your Spanish name right.
It's neither the words nor the awkward metaphor;
You delight in how the sudden shift in tone makes you laugh.
I penned a hundred more; I trust you read them all,
Before you willingly offered me your hand.
And now, we've set sail, searching for the horizon
Where the sky and the sea meet.
Last December, I met you and became a poet;
By next December, may we still be exploring the earth.

Words Fail Me
Charlene Phare

Swirling between clouds and the deep ocean
Combustible energy renewing
Extracted scents generate emotions
Pearlescent waves in grey skies ensuing
Obscure voice resonating with vision
Explosive devices causing rumours
Roads travelled excluding some precision
Division from past fusing her future
Breeze lifts this butterfly, aiding freedom
Camouflage discarded, her wings alight
Heart beats resound, natural arboretum
Conquering fears that plagued during long flights
Somewhere hovered around the sky and sea
Resembling hushed tones, that's where words fail me

a sky in fuchsia
D. A. Simpson

a sky in fuchsia adorned the heavens
where the dying sun
encountered its final hour

and a vast firmament
bore signs of weariness and frailty
at the edges of the tableau
incurred by the exertions of day

the display entire
observed by silent trees
cloaked in lachrymose attire
their mourning and sorrow
to display

while distant hills a'rolling
bathed in a light of lilac

clung to an enigmatic stillness
that abounded amid the sublime dusk light

pervading the heavens
silently melding into lavender notes
as the indigo sheet
began to unfurl across the scape
the midnight hour impending for to herald

Echoes
Gavin Prinsloo

I hear the sound from beneath the ground,
of bells that have long gone to rust,
I hear the voices of all those choices,
and bones that have turned to dust

I see the mists in which time persists,
obscuring the past within,
I see the ages within worn pages,
waiting for the past to begin

I feel the flow of what I know,
raging river within a ruptured vein,
I feel the chill of the human will,
flowing again and again

I smell the tide that time can't hide,
forever pulling me away,
I smell the past as it was cast,
upon the tide I smell today

I touch the stone over buried bone,
yet I cannot see the past,
No sight of eye nor can ears defy,
the memory of that not meant to last

Under Your Eyelids
Michael Balner

Under your closed eyelids,
there is a strange dream,
a story in a language
that you don't know how to read.

A mighty ancient pine tree
that rises high above,
its branches—searching arms—
lift the lead-heavy clouds.

The black stains of your sorrow
spoil your snow-white sheets,
and the landscape here reminds you of
nothing you have seen;

Cut in two by a lazy river
like a fresh gaping wound,
a stream filled with thick black tar
lit by a strange, wan moon.

You can choose to die here,
amidst moaning ghosts,
drown right here, night after night,
until you drown no more.

But if you dare to lift your mask,
and show me your true face,
then you shall touch my rising veins,
feel my heart's steady pace.

The rest of it is up to you,
just listen to your heart,
you can stay or leave it all behind,
it's your story to write.

The Unseen Presence of Love
Julie Loonat

The unseen presence of love
Weaves the magic in the spheres above,
Keeps the planets rotating
And the stars scintillating.

The unseen presence of love
Makes the trees
Aspire to regions higher,
Makes the tides of life ebb and flow
And the flowers open and glow.

The unseen presence of love
Keeps us anchored
In our sovereignty
And transmutes us into Divinity.

Shattered
Charlene Phare

We wade through the whispers
Swirling round in silence
Falling in the forest
The wilderness blisters
Layers broken, we're shattered
Bevelled mirror into shards
Sharpened edges thrown about
Like we never really mattered
Hold the shrapnel to the light
Lift a piece to see it shine
Its pearlescent tones spreading
It's the most beautiful sight

Two by Two
Paul Barrett

Two by two we boarded the ark;
a safe-house built of Gopher wood.
I looked for you, but it was dark

and time was short. We'd soon embark
for promised, safer neighbourhoods.
Two by two we boarded. The ark

was huge but housed no germ, no shark—
we left them where the sinners stood.
I looked for you, but it was dark

and there were howls and growls and barks
at clouds above, engorged with blood.
Two by two we boarded the ark

and prayed a coloured bow would arc
beyond the borders of the flood.
I looked for you, but it was dark

and God had long since set his mark
and then He saw that it was good.
Two by two we boarded the ark
I looked for you, but it was dark.

Washed Away
The Madd Raven

I don't think my love for you
could ever be washed away
If that were true
all my tears would have surely led the way
followed by every evening prayer I'd pray

The ocean waves upon my skin
seem to rub salt in all my wounds
And the softest wind kisses my cheek
reminds me of our love-spent afternoons
where we would run to hide our love
behind a bed of dunes

The coarse sand filtered between my fingers
mimics how our time has slipped away
And the moon appears to once again say
that tomorrow is just another day

Washed away, my love for you
will never ever be
Each day is a reminder
of what once was you and me
It hovers now in my cluttered mind
so full of fantasy
and the hope of having more than this
now washed away at sea

The Sky is a Shade of Forever
Chuck Porretto

The sky is a shade of forever,
with eternity tinting the hue.
You can feel that the artist is clever,
as infinity colors the view.

And the clouds they are woven from wishes,
with desire sewn in at the seams.
Adorning the fabric are swishes,
of fantastical notions and dreams.

While the wind is a whimsical potion,
concocted from frenzy and change.
With ingredients always in motion,
and a flavor divergent in range.

The sea is a potent libation,
as it's brewed from adventure and will.
It is garnished with hope and temptation,
and is known for its penchant to thrill.

And the beach is chest full of treasure,
that is brimming with promise and trust.
And sitting on top for good measure,
is the jewellery of passion and lust.

Oh, the moon is a shimmering sculpture,
that is carved from an ivory thought.
With a glance, it inspires a culture,
as it illustrates victory wrought.

The Earth is a heavenly garden,
that is planted in splendor and awe.
Be gentle, and never ye harden,
for the coldest of winters will thaw.

For the sun, it is made of endeavor,
reinforced with resolve, through and through.
And it hangs in a sky of forever,
as infinity colors the view.

Mercy
Lonnie Budro

There was an angel last night, who stood by my bed
Her halo still glistened on wounds where she bled
Her wings were all tattered, each feather was torn
She was my guardian angel since the day I was born

She has fought legends of demons with her sword and a shield
And each were defeated, but cannot be killed
She was triumphant in battle more times than I knew
Then patiently waited, while the child in me grew

But age never conquered my addiction to sin
And defeat was no option, she battled to win
Now years of transgressions have taken their toll
Fighting time after time, defending my soul

She stood beaten and battered, and quietly stared at the floor
Prepared in an instant, to endure even more
Never once has she faltered, or has ever complained
But now weary from battle, she whispered my name

You see ...
The prayers of a mother still come with a price
So even guardian angels ask "Mercy"
When you're not being nice

To Need More Time
Matthew Burgio

Deadlines, schedules, a calendar and clock,
Meetings at work and then working at home.
Never a moment to finish this poem,
Or analyze Mozart, Haydn or Bach.
Run from the office to stores 'round the block,
My brain's in a whirl of fog, haze and foam.
I'm tired of having to hurry and roam
As part of the world's powerless flock.
It's time to stop along life's trodden path,
To stop and smell the roses by the stream.
Then put aside the stress that causes wrath
And live a life that lets a poet dream.
No deadlines, schedules, no worries no more,
Just time for my thoughts to blossom and soar.

There's a Giant Slug in Mummy
Alyson Wilson

There's a giant slug in mummy
It lives inside her chest
Its growing every single day
Making mummy have to rest.
It saps all of her energy
It's made her weak and thin
But mummy is a fighter
And says the slug won't win.

There's a giant slug in mummy
I don't know why it's there
But it's sharing mummy's body
And stealing mummy's air.
She's trying very hard for me
To laugh and smile and play

But I see her getting weaker
Every single day.

There's a giant slug in mummy
It makes her cough and wheeze
I heard another adult say
"It's a terrible disease"
It's making mummy really ill
She says she's scared to dad
The slug is getting bigger now
And making mum feel bad.

There's a giant slug in mummy
And it's making her so ill
I wish there was a special spell
Or a magic little pill
To help my mummy fight the beast
That's growing every day
Something that could kill it
And take mum's pain away.

There's a giant slug in mummy
It's growing every day
I wish that I could fight it
And make it go away.
I'm angry that it chose her,
I'm sad, eyes full of tears
I don't know fully what's going on
But I know I'm full of fear

Daddy says that mummy's tired now,
can't fight the giant slug
That mummy needs to sleep now
That I should give her one last hug.
There was a giant slug in mummy
That lived inside her chest
It's taken mummy from me now
But she's finally at rest.

October Moon
Rose Marie Streeter

Night air
brings a chill
as old man winter
hovers
in shivering shadows
of midnight...
autumn leaves
fall on their pretty faces
with their gowns torn
to shreds
from his horrid
breath...
A cough
liken to
death rattle
haunts
throughout
the night...
Yet....
when time stills
he will sleep
'fore waking to renewal
reincarnated
in bright attire
bringing new hope
with sunshine smiles
hugging the earth...

WHEELSONG POETRY ANTHOLOGY 5

About Wheelsong Books

Wheelsong Books is an independent poetry publishing
company based in the ocean city of Plymouth,
on the beautiful Southwest coast of England.
Established by poet Steve Wheeler in 2019,
the company aims to promote previously unheard voices
and encourage new talent in poetry. Wheelsong is also
the home of the Absolutely Poetry
and Invisible Poets anthology series,
featuring previously unpublished and emerging poets
from around the globe.

Wheelsong always has more poetry publications in the
pipeline! You can read more about Wheelsong Books and its
growing stable of exciting new and emerging poets on the
Wheelsong Books website at: wheelsong.co.uk

Wheelsong publication list

2020
Ellipsis by Steve Wheeler
Inspirations by Kenneth Wheeler
Sacred (2020, Revised 2024) by Steve Wheeler
Living by Faith by Kenneth Wheeler
Urban Voices by Steve Wheeler

2021
Small Lights Burning by Steve Wheeler
My Little Eye by Steve Wheeler
Ascent (2021, Revised 2023) by Steve Wheeler
Dance of the Metaphors by Rafik Romdhani
Into the Grey by Brandon Adam Haven
RITE by Steve Wheeler
Absolutely Poetry Anthology 1 by various

2022
Absolutely Poetry Anthology 2 by various
War Child by Steve Wheeler
Hoyden's Trove by Jane Newberry
Shocks and Stares by Steve Wheeler
Autumn Shedding by Christian Ryan Pike
Cobalt Skies by Charlene Phare
Wheelsong Poetry Anthology 1 by various
Rough Roads by Rafik Romdhani

2023
Symphoniya de Toska: Book One by Marten Hoyle
Vapour of the Mind by Rafik Romdhani
Nocturne by Steve Wheeler
Symphoniya de Toska: Book Two by Marten Hoyle
Wheelsong Poetry Anthology 2 by various
Constellation Road by Matthew Elmore
Beyond the Pyre by Imelda Zapata Garcia

Symphoniya de Toska: Book Three by Marten Hoyle
Wheelsong Poetry Anthology 3 by various
This Broken House by Brandon Adam Haven

2024
All the Best (Poetry 2020-2023) by Steve Wheeler
Invisible Poets Anthology 1 by Invisible Poets
Darkness into Light by David Catterton Grantz
Wheelsong Poetry Anthology 4 by various
Marmalade Hue by Donna Marie Smith
Melancholy Moon by Gregory Richard Barden
Average Angel by Matthew Elmore
The Infinite Now by Steve Wheeler
Storming Oblivion Peter Rivers
Stealing Fire by Tyrone M. Warren
Wheelsong Poetry Anthology 5 by various
Circus of Circles by Aoife Cunningham
Invisible Poets Anthology 2 by Invisible Poets

The **Wheelsong Poetry Anthology** series – raising funds for Save the Children worldwide relief fund.

These and all other titles are available for purchase in paperback, and Kindle editions and some in hardcover on Amazon.com, direct from wheelsong.co.uk or by emailing the publisher at: wheelsong6@gmail.com

Printed in Great Britain
by Amazon